SPORE™

Written By Rusel DeMaria

MAXIS™   EA

AS WE BEGIN OUR LATEST **ASTOUNDING SPORE TALE**, A MYSERIOUS OBJECT HURTLES TOWARDS THE DENSE ATMOSPHERE OF XANALDONN XII...

astounding Spore tales

HAVING TRAVELED MILLIONS OF LIGHT YEARS, THE UNUSUAL PROJECTILE APPEARS ALMOST ANXIOUS TO REACH ITS DESTINATION...

FROM THE SURFACE OF THE PLANET, THE OBJECT APPEARS TO BE A COMET OR PERHAPS A FALLING STAR...

SUDDENLY, THE OBJECT MAKES A SHARP RIGHT TURN AND...

KRAKK-A-THOM

...THE SOUND BARRIER IS **SHATTERED!!!**

THE TERRIFYING SOUND IMMEDIATELY DRAWS THE ATTENTION OF THE UNSUSPECTING INHABITANTS OF XANALDONN XII.

THEY MARVEL IN FEAR AT A SIGHT YET UNSEEN BY THEIR YOUNG CIVILIZATION.

MEANWHILE, DEEP WITHIN THE HOLLOW CORE OF THE UNIDENTIFIED PROJECTILE, WE DISCOVER THAT IT IS NO MERE CELESTIAL ANOMALY...

MY FAITHFUL MINIONS... I, **GLOKK THE DESTROYER** HAVE LED YOU ACROSS THE UNIVERSE TO THIS DAY...

I created *Amazing Spore Tales* as both an homage to the '30s and '40s sci-fi pulp magazines that I love as well as a vehicle for observing what *Spore* would look like in the public conscious. Seeing *Spore* on a magazine cover while we were still very early in production made the whole thing seem more real and somewhat tangible. The popularity of the cover work led to requests for a story to go along with it, so I came up with a four-pager in order to flesh the idea out entirely.

—Bob King, Director of Animation

Introduction by Will Wright

I'm ready to be interviewed. All I can tell you is name, rank, and serial number.

The initial idea for *Spore*™ came out of the SETI program, the search for extraterrestrial intelligence, which led me to Drake's Equation and astrobiology, especially because there was a lot of stuff happening in these sciences, where people are now, for the first time, discovering extra-solar planets and learning more about the basic genesis of life. And in the area of astrobiology I find Drake's Equation fascinating, especially when you look at the terms: how many stars are in a galaxy, how many of those have planets, how many of those form life, how many of those life forms become a higher order, or become intelligent. These terms hit all these different scales, all these different fields of science. They hit physics, chemistry, cosmology, astronomy—even things like sociology and economics.

At the same time, I've always been really interested in the Powers of 10 idea, which is really just a way of looking at the universe on all these different scales, and it occurred to me that the different terms in Drake's Equation, which represent these different fields of science, mapped very nicely to the different scales of the Powers of 10. And so those two things roughly came together on the thematic side of *Spore*. And on the other side, I was observing what our players were doing with *The Sims*™—creating cool content, sharing it through websites, making collections, telling stories. And so that was another side of it; the content side of *Spore* was very much influenced by *Sims* players and by observing their meta-play dynamics.

The first prototypes for *Spore* were created right after *The Sims* was released. Another inspiration behind *Spore* was my feeling that galaxies are these very cool, beautiful, amazing things of vast size and diversity,

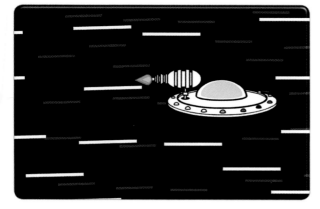

This picture is the very first image I'd done of *Spore*, back in 2002, I'm thinkin', or early in 2003 when I had my first conversations with Will. We were both working on *The Sims Online*. I was the art director, and I kind of realized that he had something else on his mind and that there was going to be a "next thing." We went to lunch. So I asked, "What have you got going on?" And of course he talked to me all about powers of ten, molecular levels. He's always been very interested in space games and traveling the universe and things, but I'm [the] animator/character guy, and I was trying to ask him questions about creatures.... But he hadn't really given it much thought at that point, and I'm like, well, if I was going to make something—I thought about the toys I played with as a kid and [how if] I was going to be able to make this planet that had creatures, and everything on it was going to be made by me—what would it look like? So I came up with this, drawing as he was talking, and touched it up a little bit later. I kind of held onto it, and held onto it, in the back of my head thinking, "This is going to be interesting, and at some point, some day, somebody's going to want to know about this."

—Bob King, Director of Animation

and I always wanted to have a toy galaxy to play with. I loved the idea of having a toy galaxy to explore. I wanted to not only show how vast and beautiful it is, but also to represent the kinds of things you would find in a galaxy— things you would see in the Hubble space telescope. Most people look at these photos and they have no sense of reference, no sense of scale. So you see a planetary nebula and you see an emissive nebula like Orion that seems like roughly the same thing, but you have no point of reference to even compare the two, to show that one is vastly larger than the other. So having a toy galaxy—this cosmological zoo where you can go in and see these weird objects and appreciate their density and how large and frequent they are—is a nice way to start developing an intuition for a system in which we actually live but that is quite removed from our familiar frame of reference.

I think from the reading I've done in this area—I've lost count of how many books and articles I've read at this point—I'm convinced that we're most likely the only intelligent life form in our galaxy, for a lot of reasons. But that makes for a relatively boring game. So there are some places where I totally split with my intuition of what reality is versus reality in our game. It might be science fiction. It might turn out to be science fact, compared with what I think is true, but I don't necessarily want to impose creatorial opinions, or this kind of message, in the form of a dogmatic, "No. There shall be no other intelligent life in our galaxy." And in any case, it wouldn't be fun, and if it's not fun, then any message you try and embed in it is wasted, you know? And even if I really did want to convince people of that, I wouldn't do it by making a boring game. "Look how boring the galaxy is going to be when you get out there." You know? I think there are intelligent life forms out there. I just think they are really far away.

In fact, according to some theories, there are three possible states of our galaxy, which we've created prototypes to experiment with. One state is where life is microbial, and microbes can spread through the galaxy, through space (panspermia). The next state is where life becomes complex, multicellular, and yet not sufficiently technological to leave its planet, which means life will not spread in that state. Then there's the intelligent state where you might have creatures in spaceships, and life can spread in that state. I think we're in the middle state. There's one point at which most of our galaxy has a lot of systems alive with microbial life, and there's some point at which intelligence springs up in it. And I think that's right where we're at, based upon the data that we've seen. I think that's the highest likelihood.

I think we'll make it out to the next stage, though. I think the next couple of hundred of years or so are going to be critical, but if we can get past that I think we're going to fill the galaxy with our offspring in very short order (20 million years, give or take). And they'll probably be more mechanical (or engineered biological). I think it will be engineered intelligences that we build to go out and basically colonize the galaxy. It's basically more efficient than having biological humans traveling on ships. I mean, humans should be able to transcend their physical limitations through technology, through machines. For instance, if you could download your consciousness into a computer, then send yourself off to the nearest star system, you could put yourself on pause for 10,000 years, and it's not going to be nearly as boring a trip, as opposed to an organic life form that has to live through 50 generations, explaining to the kids why they are going to be born and die on a starship, just so their great-great-great-great grandkids can reach this place. So it doesn't really make a lot of sense for organic life forms to be flying around the stars, but once you begin to transcend our basic evolved, biological limitations, it's actually quite convenient.

So a lot of our first steps involved figuring out the scope of the game, how far up and down we were

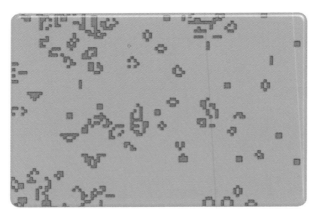

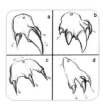

ORIGINAL

possible variations of the scale trees to be used in the various editors in Spore

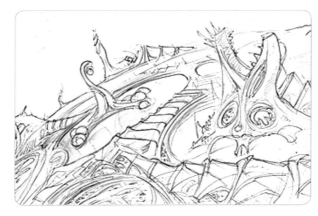

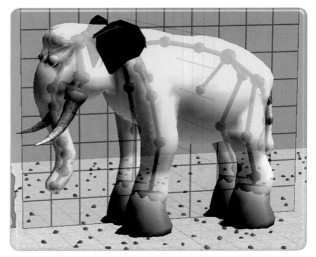

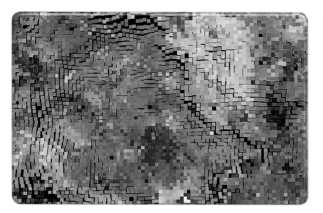

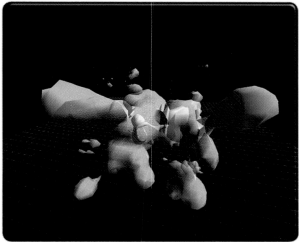

going to go in scale, what dynamics we were going to simulate at each level, how we make this experience into a cohesive whole—that was on the design side. On the technology side, from the beginning it was rather obvious that we were going to have to do almost everything with procedural generation because of the vast scope of the assets we would be dealing with. And going down that path, as we started playing with some of the procedural techniques and technologies, we also wanted to give players the ability to make as much of the world as possible. Those went pretty much hand in hand. If the computer could make the assets then it would be easier for the player to make the assets, and the assets would be very compressible (and hence transportable). So there was a lot of synergy between these specific technologies, but we had to dig into it and research them to a level that hadn't really been done up to this point in games or in academia.

From the very beginning the evolution of life was intended to be the core of the game; realistically exploring stars and nebula probably has limited interest for most people. We really wanted you to go explore and experience all these diverse, alien life forms. Probably the most interesting thing that players will be creating in *Spore* will be weird, alien creatures. From that, then you can start imagining, "What would their buildings look like? Their vehicles? Their starships? Planets?" It makes the other stuff more interesting, once you have your protagonist. So the evolution part was in there from the beginning. At the very beginning, though, we were originally looking at a game where you were dealing with large creatures evolving and going out to the stars, and at some point (that's where the powers of 10 idea came in), we thought, "Let's go further back to the beginning of life, and let's start at the microscopic level."

In fact, in many of our early prototypes we went further down than that. We were at the autocatalytic chemistry level. We did several prototypes involving molecular and organic chemistry that ended up not making it into the game. In fact at one point we considered starting the player at the atomic level. There were other prototypes we made of toy chemistries, with those toy chemistries eventually turning into organic chemistries, and those organic chemistries turning into autocatalytic sets, and autocatalytic sets then bootstrapping into the first cellular life forms. So that was a whole section of the game that we cut out. But most people are more comfortable starting at a less zoomed-in level of the powers of 10, because cells (life) are inherently more interesting than atoms to most people. The chemistry prototypes were fun to play with if you knew what they were. And some of the autocatalytic stuff we did was pretty cool, too, but it's geeky.

Probably the biggest challenge was the design challenge of making all these genres of gameplay feel like a cohesive whole. And alongside that, the biggest technical challenge was in general the procedural assets, and the specific techniques like procedural animation. That was probably the hardest part of the game from the technical standpoint. The procedural texturing mesh geometry was quite a bit simpler. Procedural music ended up being not quite as hard as we thought it would be. It was something that came in somewhat late to the game when Brian Eno joined the project. The level of detail (LOD) graphics and simulation engine was also a major technical challenge because we're simulating, in some sense, an entire galaxy. As you go out and explore space, at any given time we're simulating one or two planets at a high resolution, maybe a hundred planets at low resolution, and on that high-resolution planet you can zoom in to one individual creature and look at exactly where his foot is moving. And so there are various levels of detail being both simulated and rendered depending on

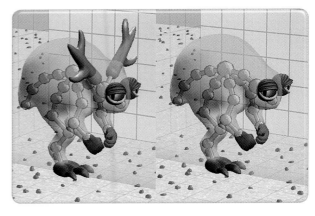

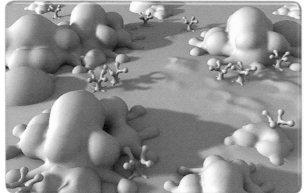

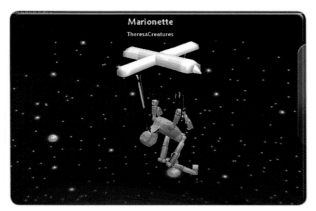

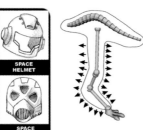

exactly where you are.

Pollination was an idea that came up early in the project. As we started building the game creators, getting some sense of how amazingly freeform they were going to be and how interesting the results would be, then it was totally natural to say, "Oh, we want to share these things." Also, we had to populate an immense galaxy for each player. How could we possibly populate a vast galaxy with thousands of worlds without the pollination? So in some sense, once we bit off the galaxy, we were committing ourselves to something like pollination. Despite the obvious community value, I think it was more of a pragmatic feature, because once we said we were going to do a galaxy, it was like "Oh, crap. How are we going to populate it? Oh, I get it. We can get the players to help us." So, from the beginning we knew we'd have to do something like this, and then it was a matter of how deep do we go down that path to refine the concept.

So what I hope for this game is that average people who don't necessarily care that much about science will be able to take five big steps back and have this vast perspective on life and the universe. In some sense I hope it will inspire some players to contemplate how we got to be where we are, and where we might go in the future. It's an unusual view of the history and the future of life. So I think that is probably the most important part for me. I think most people at some point or another have glimpsed this idea, perhaps looking up at the stars on a clear summer night, but not typically to this level. It's one thing to have these vague feelings of awe and wonder at the scope of the galaxy and how long we've been on Earth, but it's another thing entirely to actually play it through and experience it multiple times. I think it gives you a more refined sense of the value of life, and how unique life is, really, relative to everything else. I think that is, for me, the highest aspiration I have for *Spore*.

  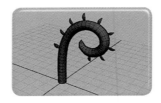   

I have lesser aspirations, too. I think when people find tools that allow them to be creative to levels that they've never been before, they find it very empowering. That is one of the coolest things about computers, that computers can enable people to make things and build imaginative constructs, stories, or whatever, that they wouldn't do otherwise. It's very much like the way in which a pencil enables some people to become artists or an instrument enables others to become musicians. So in some sense the computer's highest use in my mind is to allow us to further develop our imaginary worlds; an amplifier for our imagination if you will.

I think a lot of people hopefully won't really think of *Spore* as a game; they'll think of it as this elaborate toy box or creativity tool, or a place they go to make cool, unique, interesting worlds, and then watch what happens and play with the results. Some players will probably view it as a galactic terrarium. I think for some, even the concept of a game is not as appealing as a really fun toy that turns into a tool. *Spore* is probably gamier than *The Sims*. It has real goals to achieve and progress that's measured, but at the same time it's probably a more open-ended sandbox than *The Sims*. But one of the real design challenges is to make sure the game doesn't overly influence the toy and that the toy doesn't overly dilute the game—that they can play well together.

So what is the distinction between "toy" and "game"? A toy is something with interesting dynamics that encourages you to come in and interact with it. You can choose to create games with it or you might even use it for pure freeform play, or it can also potentially evolve into a tool, let's say for communication or self-expression. So I think of "toy" as a much more foundational, almost more abstract concept than a game, which feels more specific. For instance, you can place various goals on a toy and turn it into a game, but you can also just play with it and develop intuitions, or you can play with it and you can actually have some output. I can play with an Etch-A-Sketch and create a piece of art on it. Or I can sit there and just take it apart and see how it works, where for the most part I think people would define a game as having a formal goal state, not necessarily win or lose, and associated rules.

There were certain core people who were influential in the very early stages, because the first year or two of *Spore* involved a handful of four or five people who did a lot of the early prototypes, and I want to make sure they get credited at the that level. So Jason Shankel was the first person on *Spore*, and he did a lot of the earliest prototypes. He, in fact, was working on an early project of ours called *SimMars*, which got canceled. So a lot of the ideas that came in on the planetary level of detail—how we visualize things and simulate things—were subtly influenced by *SimMars* or previous work. Chris Trottier, my codesigner on *The Sims Online*, was instrumental on the design side, always making sure we didn't go down the geeky, science path too far. Ed Goldman was another one. He's not on the product now, but he was for many years. He was actually my lead programmer for *SimCopter*™ and *SimCity Urban Renewal Kit*™, so he was one of the guys I had worked with for many years. Chaim Gingold, my intern originally from Georgia Tech, did a lot of the early prototyping. Brad Smith was another intern who came in and did a lot of the very first creator work. So the very first creature creators were all Brad's work. And of course our art director, Ocean Quigley, ongoing from day one had a huge impact on the visual style and also on how we could deconstruct things, like creature parts, into the animation channels, working behind the scenes and understanding, from an engineer's point of view and an artist's point of view, how to make the ends meet. Another guy who was on the early team, Kees van Prooijen, did many of the prototypes, like the one where we have a little guy animating on a surface to test movement with different dynamics. He was the first guy to actually dig into the animation system, and did some of the earliest work where the creature could actually move around and walk, which later got picked up by "Checker" (Chris Hecker), who expanded it and built other tools. And then of course Lucy Bradshaw coming in on the organizational side. So then there were several people working on these prototypes in the early days, working with me, slowly refining....You know, of the hundred possible ideas that *Spore* could have become, slowly refining down to the one idea that *Spore* was going to become was a lot of exploration, and I can't even begin to tell you how many prototypes we built during that exploration stage.

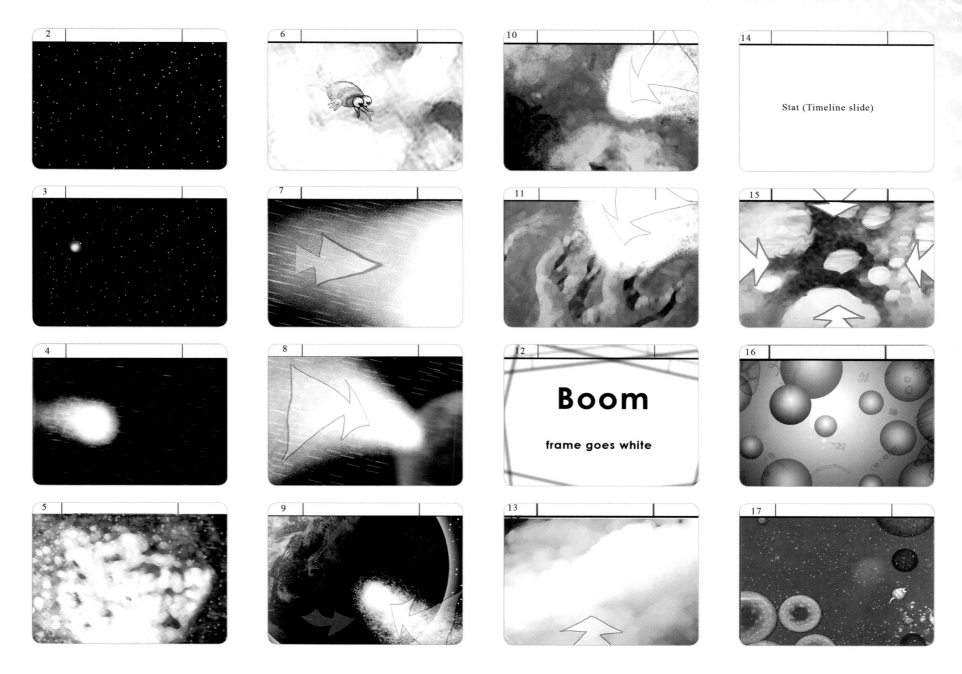

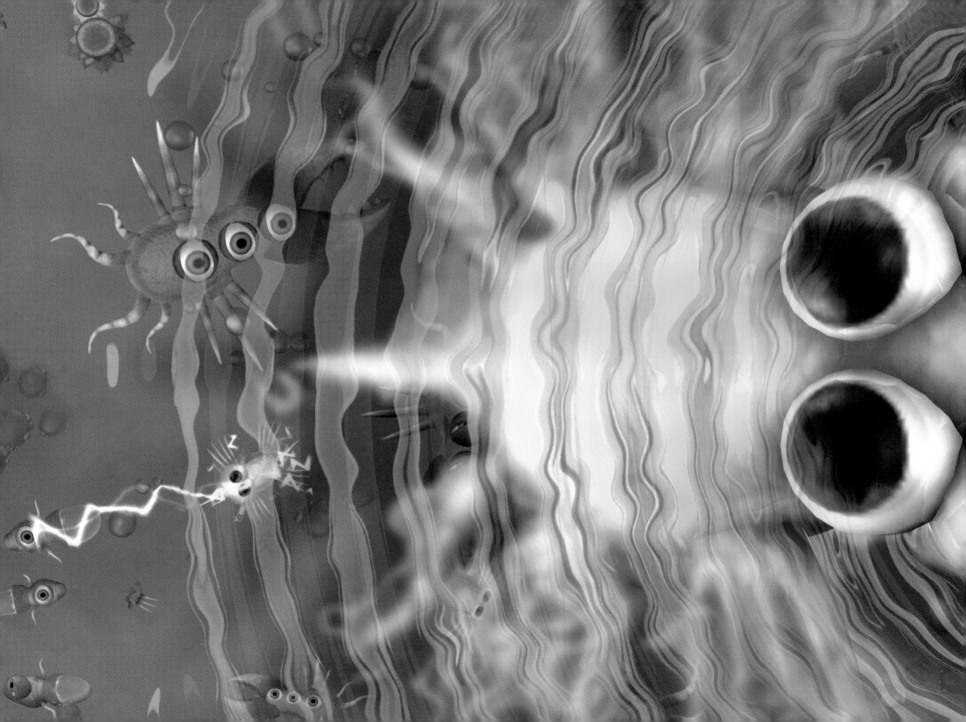

cell
stage

The Cell game is meant to be an introduction to the game of *Spore* and to life itself. Right off the bat, the player is fighting to survive, grow, and reproduce. We wanted to give the player a familiar game setting—2D, 360-degree scroller—in which to introduce the basic concepts of *Spore* gameplay, most notably the process of zooming up in scale and using the Creators.

—Will Wright, *Spore* Vision & Chief Designer

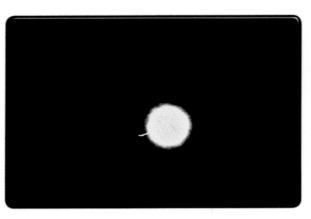

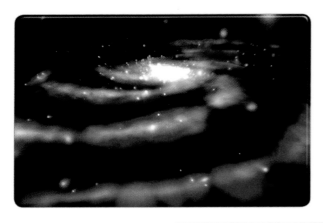

Evolution of a Cell

Our first contact with *Spore* occurs when a space-borne microbe encapsulated in a meteor hits the planet. This is where our journey begins.

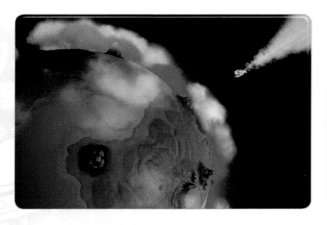

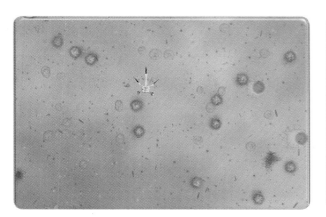

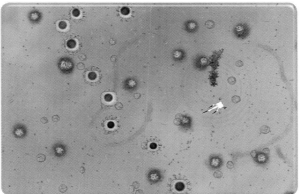

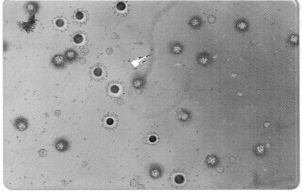

Originally, *Spore* was going to start at the subatomic level, and so Will did some prototypes that were about autocatalytic sets. They were basically games where you would assemble a self-replicating molecule, but we decided that it was just too small in scale and too hard to empathize with. We thought maybe we should start with life instead of the chemical precursors to life, and so I did a prototype in our original animation viewer.

At that time we hadn't really done anything with Cell game, and it looked like it might fall by the wayside, so I hacked together a quick prototype. In the creature creator, for instance, you could make a creature about the size of a cow. I built an environment around it that made it look like a tiny creature in a world of cellular goop, which you can see in the screenshots.

This was the prototype that Will demoed at GDC in 2005. That's the cool thing about these effects prototypes. We were able to do some really convincing demos. That whole GDC demo was really a strung-together series of prototypes meant to give a big picture of what the game would be like.

—OCEAN QUIGLEY, ART DIRECTOR

My original idea for the Cell game was, "big fish eats little fish." And the basic play idea was based more or less on Pac-Man™, where you go around eating things and trying to avoid being eaten by the ghosts—in this case, the "big fish."

—OCEAN QUIGLEY, ART DIRECTOR

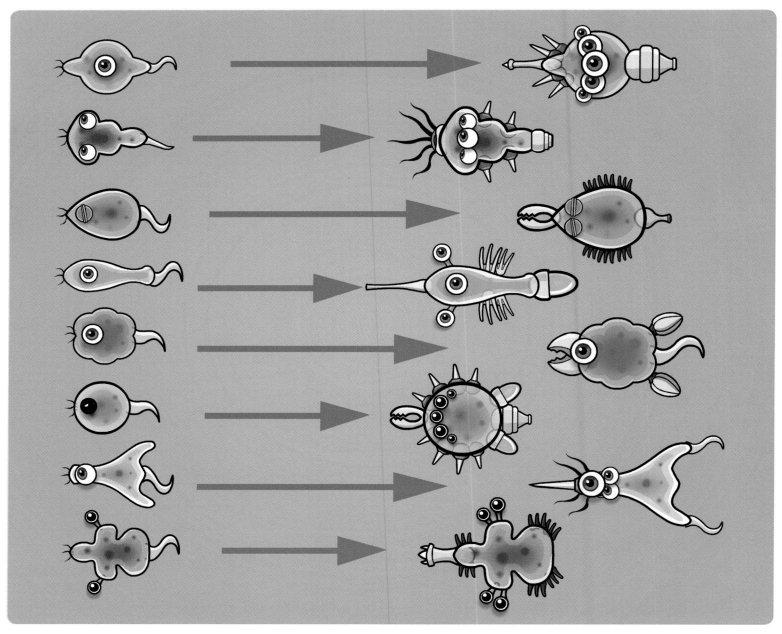

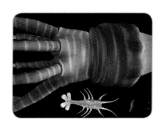

Once my Cell game prototype was done, [artist] Shannon Galvin had the idea to make growth across all the scales of the Cell game be one of the arcs of the game. So you start out tiny and get bigger and bigger and bigger until you get to the size of an animal. And that became one of the defining aspects of the Cell game—growth through scale. This neatly bookends the game with the Space game, providing a counterpoint for the universal scale you have at the end.
—Ocean Quigley, Art Director

 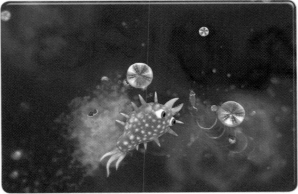 

A couple of ideas followed from the idea of scale. One was that we could make the landscape out of creatures that are vastly larger than you. Rather than creating some kind of fixed world, like a maze with walls and doors, we created a world out of the creatures in it. To a flea, a dog is a massive mountain range. To a little cellular creature, a small fish is a continent. So the environment was actually the life within it.

—Ocean Quigley, Art Director

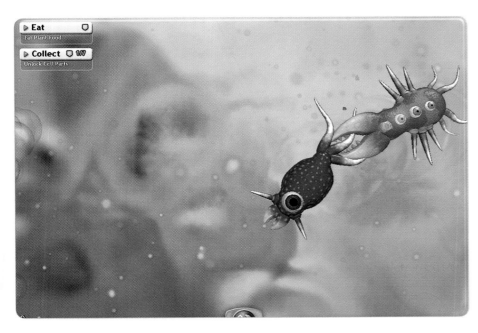 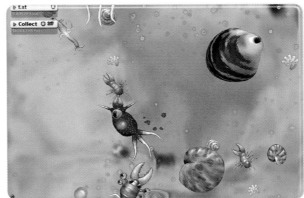

As you get bigger and bigger, your relationship to the other creatures changes. First you get bullied, then you're competing with other bullies for victims, and then you get to be the bully. But there's always another bully bigger than you.

Put another way, the creatures that are initially hunting you, your predators, eventually become your prey.

—Ocean Quigley, Art Director

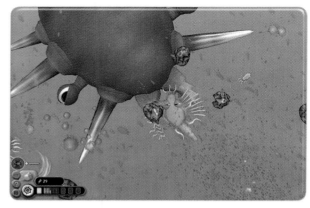

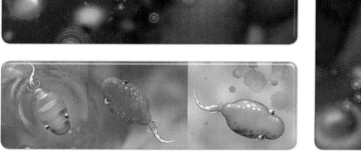

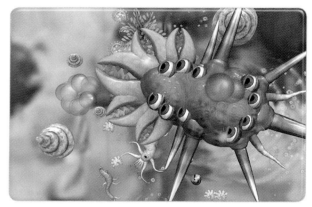

One of our key visual touchstones was the aesthetic of microscopy. So you start out very small and you have this very narrow range of focus. Everything above you is blurry; everything below you is blurry. There's only a narrow sliver that is in focus. And that depth of field, relative sharpness versus blurriness, would be one of the signifiers of scale. As you grow larger, your area of focus increases and what was once your whole world is now merely a speck.

Along with the aesthetic of microscopy came the idea of transparency. At your smallest you are essentially transparent, but as you get bigger and the creatures around you get bigger, they become more and more opaque. This is another way of visually demonstrating your progress and movement through the scales of the game.

—Ocean Quigley, Art Director

Swimming into the current, not making any progress, but my parts all stick out straight, rather than being pushed behind me.

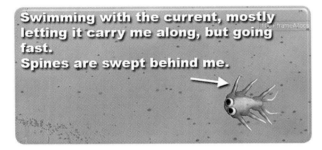

Swimming with the current, mostly letting it carry me along, but going fast.
Spines are swept behind me.

The images on this page represent the use of currents in the tide pool to create a more lively and interesting environment for the player's cell creature. As Ocean Quigley says, "It makes you feel like you're swirling and flowing in this aqueous environment, again, not like a fixed maze with walls and positioned obstacles."

In addition to creating the world around you from the creatures, we wanted the environment to feel fluid, liquid and flowing. So the other aesthetic was one of flow and movement. We made passages of turbulence, passages of smooth currents and areas of calmness. Different areas would have different qualities of movement. Some are choppy and some are smooth.

The basic currents in the Cell game were created by painting flowfields. Imagine you have a rug and a comb, and you comb the fibers of the rug in different directions. The direction of the fibers are the currents in the tide pool world of the Cell game. We could brush a fast current or a light swirling region. And to make it more organic, the larger creatures are also affecting the currents and causing perturbations that are felt by the smaller creatures. It makes you feel like you're swirling and flowing in this aqueous world, not stuck in a rigid maze with walls and positioned obstacles.

—Ocean Quigley, Art Director

The Cell Creator

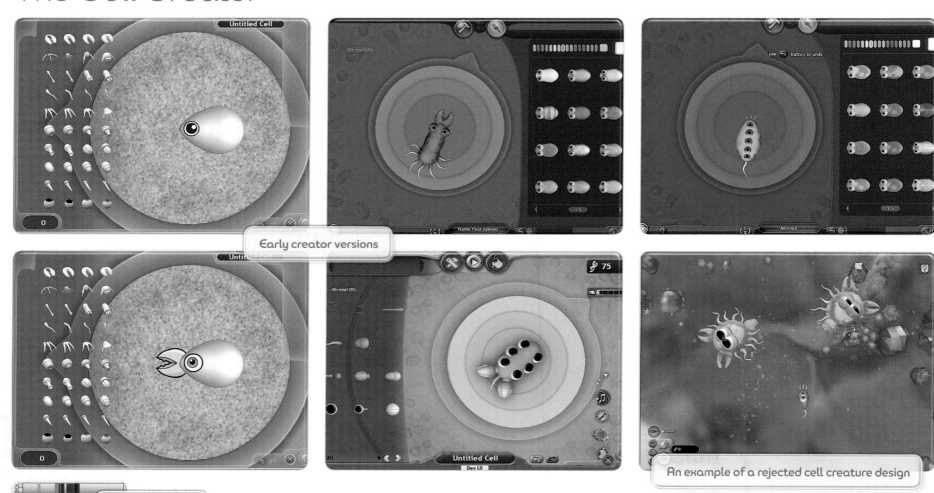

Early creator versions

An example of a rejected cell creature design

Dev UI

Color coding for the Cell Stage

Will wanted to make the Cell game function as an entrance to the Creature game, preparing players for what they would do as creatures, both in the gameplay and in the creators.

With the Cell Creator, the player has a simplified version of the Creature Creator so they can get used to the way it works, to the nouns and verbs of the system. It's like a tutorial so when players get to the Creature Creator, they'll say, "Oh, I know what to do here."

—Ocean Quigley, Art Director

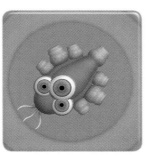

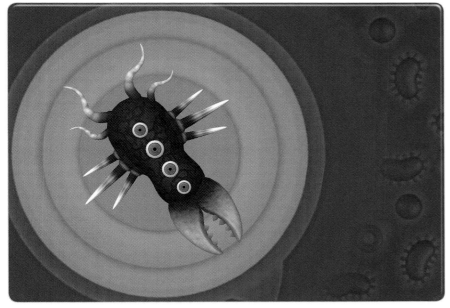

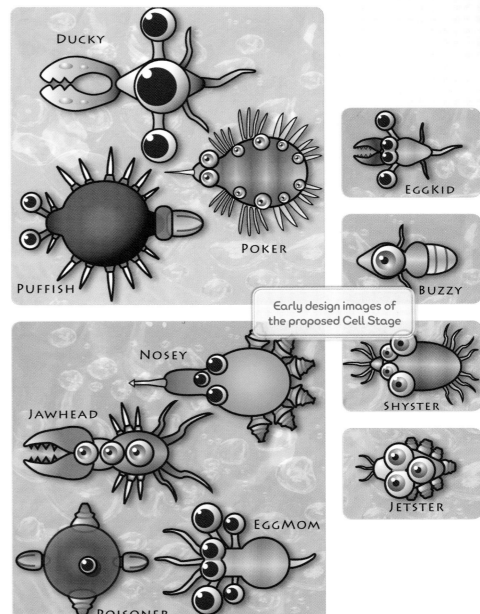

DUCKY

EGGKID

PUFFISH

POKER

BUZZY

Early design images of
the proposed Cell Stage

NOSEY

SHYSTER

JAWHEAD

JETSTER

POISONER

EGGMOM

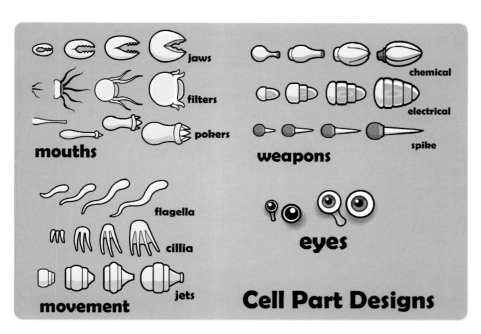

mouths
jaws
filters
pokers

flagella

cilia

movement
jets

Cell Part Designs

weapons
chemical
electrical
spike

eyes

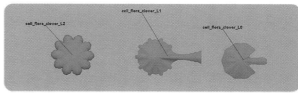

cell_flora_clover_L2
cell_flora_clover_L1
cell_flora_clover_L0

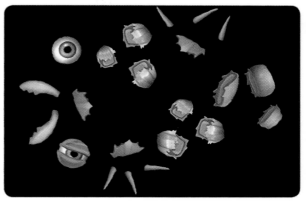

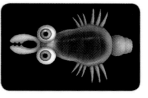

In terms of animation. Cell game was a different problem from the other levels. The cells are so inherently simple and fish-like that it made it a little tricky for me to convey emotion. Normally, I would make the creatures act by posing and moving their heads and arms around, but here I was pretty much completely reliant on moving around the root. It's kind of like a little kid animating an action figure in his hand and just shaking it all around to show emotion. If the Cell creature is scared, I open his eyes wide and shake it about.

—John Cimino, Animator

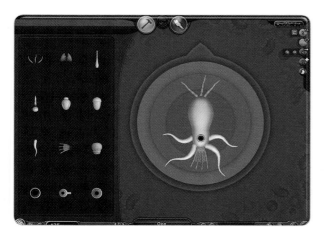

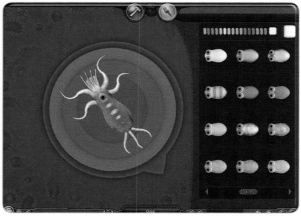

From the gameplay perspective. Will wanted to make the Cell game function as an entrance into the Creature game, essentially preparing players for what they would have to do as creatures, both in the gameplay and in the creators. With the Cell Creator, the player is presented with a simplified version of the Creature Creator so they can get used to the way it works, to the nouns and verbs of the system. It acts like a tutorial so that when they get to the Creature Creator, they'll say, "Oh, I know what to do here."

—Ocean Quigley, Art Director

The Lost Level

Originally, there was going to be an underwater level before you got onto land, a sort of fish level. We even prototyped it, and it was shown in storyboards at GDC, but ultimately we decided to bail on it.

The main reason was navigation. In the Cell game you were operating in a 2-D space, essentially navigating on a plane. In the Creature game, the ground acts as a plane. But in the underwater game, you were in a volume, where you would have to navigate in 3-D. It was like a flight model. So navigation put the kibosh on the underwater game, even though our early prototypes looked pretty nice, with shafts of light spearing through the water and some nice underwater effects. But that was abandoned and now we go directly from the Cell game to the Creature game

—Ocean Quigley, Art Director

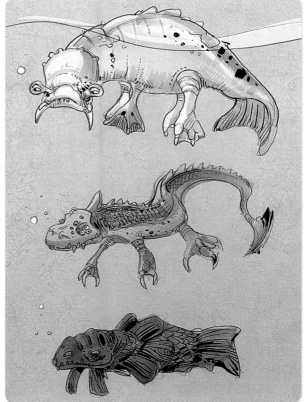

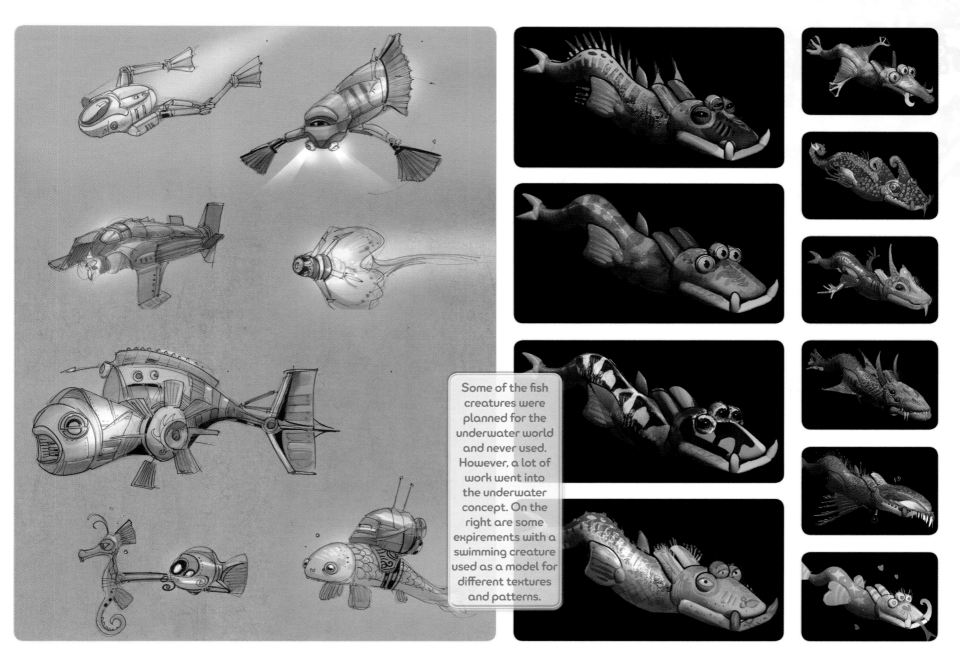

Some of the fish creatures were planned for the underwater world and never used. However, a lot of work went into the underwater concept. On the right are some expirements with a swimming creature used as a model for different textures and patterns.

There was even a proposed world with elaborate underwater landscapes and cities.

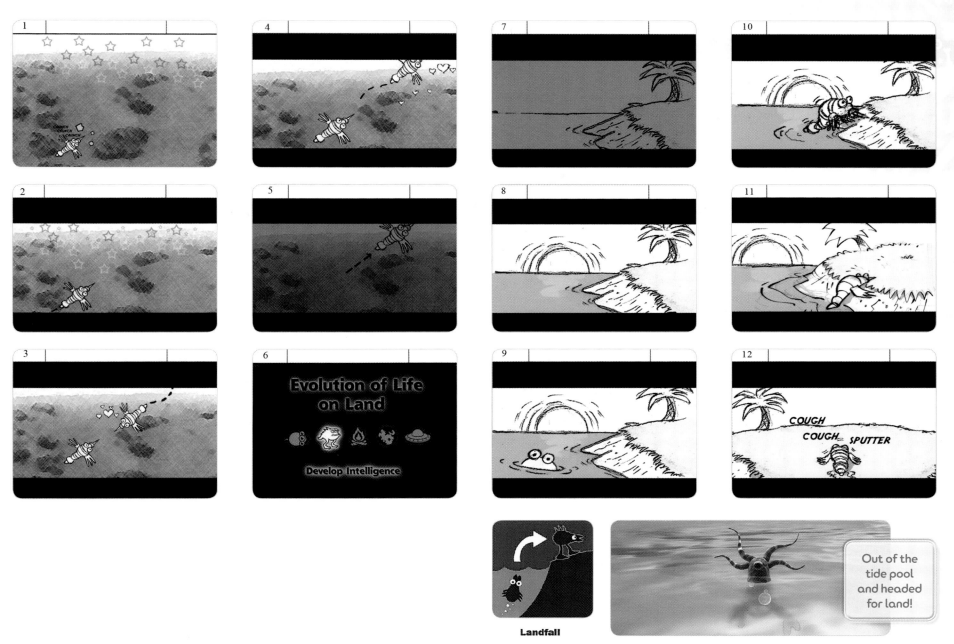

Landfall

Out of the tide pool and headed for land!

2 creature stage

Early in development it became obvious to me that the Creature game was going to be the star of the show in many ways—it integrates the strongest creator, and it lets you get close to your creations as well as have the opportunity to meet an endless stream of other player's creations up close and personal.

—Alex Hutchinson,
Lead Designer: Gameplay

The Creature Challenge

The Creature Stage was critical to the vision of *Spore*, and both the philosophy and the methodology of the game met with initial challenges. How the *Spore* team tackled those challenges has produced this remarkable and unique experience.

Typically we try to make as much use of the existing programming as we can. By existing programming, I mean things the player already knows. So typically we will try to give them fairly successful metaphors when we present them with something. We say, this is like clay or this is like Mr. Potato Head, or this is like Tinker Toys, or this is like *Pac-Man* or paper-rock-scissors. And so we hang off existing concepts that they have and then just elaborate on those. That way they can already bring an existing model to the game. That way it's simpler off the bat, even though if you look at the absolute complexity of it, it might be fairly high.... So just as with a toy, as soon as you begin to interact with it you have to be able to touch and manipulate and play with this thing, and enjoy the discovery process. And so, if there is complexity, we want the discovery of that complexity to be enjoyable, and not something where you have to break open and study manuals before you understand what to do, before you start playing the game.

—WILL WRIGHT, *SPORE* VISION & CHIEF DESIGNER

Will Wright: Is he really a *Spore* creature? Inquiring minds want to know.

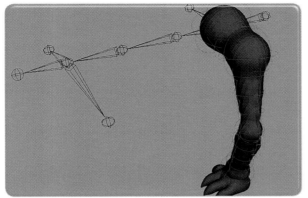

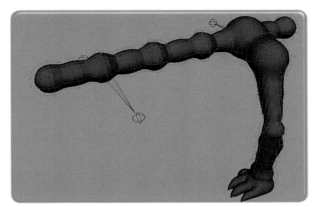

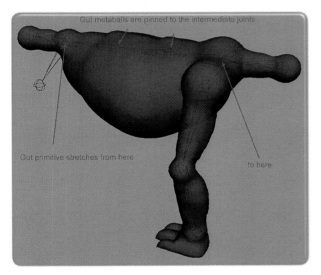

Gut metaballs are pinned to the intermediate joints

Gut primitive stretches from here

to here

Initially, because we wanted the game to be very different, and very procedural, and very based upon users' creativity, we faced a number of technical issues about how to be both procedural and innovative—procedural texturing, and things like that. And the initial team members I brought along were to mitigate those risks. Basically these were the things that had not really been solved, or had not been done before, and I wanted to be sure we could actually solve these problems. So the very first people were pretty deep technologists looking into these problems and whether we could solve them.

—WILL WRIGHT, SPORE VISION & CHIEF DESIGNER

"In some sense we're designing five different games that all have to mesh together very smoothly and share common controls and common user interface."

—WILL WRIGHT, SPORE VISION & CHIEF DESIGNER

Gameplay

The challenge in creating the Creature game is that if you say that players can make virtually any creature they can imagine, and the other creatures that they meet, which usually provide the challenges in a game, are made by other players and they can also be massively varied, and finally you say that the world has to support five different types of games in the same environment which means you can't control it's structure very much, then you start waking up in a cold sweat as you realize you've created a massive challenge for yourself as a designer. We realized at that point that we didn't know what the player's character was, who the other characters in the world were, or what the

world was shaped like, which basically removed the three basic tools designers have—control of those three elements is how you make a game. So we had to ask ourselves, "How can we create rules and archetypes that will help give us structure?"
—Alex Hutchinson, Lead Designer: Gameplay

Instead of just saying, "Here's a series of jumping puzzles or here's a sequence of progressively more difficult enemies to fight," we are saying, "Do whatever you want, and we will try to do the hard work of making a game around you." This is also the key to the creators, where we basically say, "Do whatever you want and we will make it work. Put the legs where you want, put as many eyes on—we'll make it work." The key is making the creator open and expansive as opposed to constrictive.
—Alex Hutchinson, Lead Designer: Gameplay

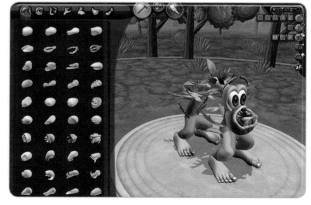

Really I think for us to be successful with this project, we need to enable the player's personal fiction. Players need to have a connection with what they are building, and they need to feel that how they develop their species matters.

—Matt Powers, Producer: Gameplay

Another fun issue we had was trying to reconcile what Will thought was the core story of the Creature Stage—gaining intelligence and evolving an entire species—against what players tended to think during play, which was that they had a unique creature that was continually mutating. So even though the game they are playing represents the evolution of their species over a long period, people consistently felt that it was the story of a single avatar over a short period. Players are used to playing persistent characters, and this was typical of the problems we would face. We found ourselves running up against commonly accepted ideas of how a game should play, or some commonly held idea about what a game avatar is, which meant we had to try and teach our players to think in different ways.

The core example of this kind of problem occurred with the user controls. From the very get-go the vision was five different—quite different—games which unfortunately meant we also ended up with five different control schemes, and when we tried to blend them into a single, unified control scheme…. Well, if you try to build an RTS [real-time strategy] that has unusual controls so it's compatible with the other phases, gamers freak out. So it's been an ongoing process of refinement to get what works best without violating what people expect.

—Alex Hutchinson, Lead Designer: Gameplay

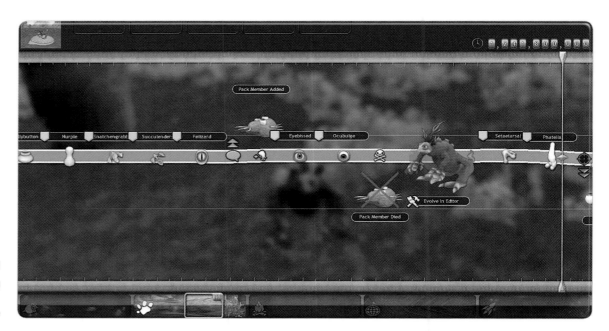

One of the last features we've added is a timeline. The purpose of the timeline is to record all the important events in the history of your play experience, like when you evolved, when you encountered other people's creations, when you defeated or socialized other races. It's dynamic, so you can access it anytime. The aim is to let people realize that when they've eventually taken their cell all the way to space that they've told a detailed story about the evolution of their creations and hopefully to make that story alive and visible and sharable.
—ALEX HUTCHINSON, LEAD DESIGNER: GAMEPLAY

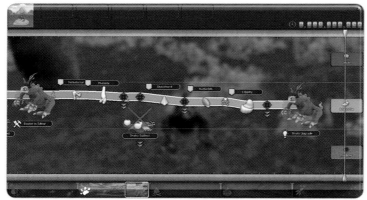

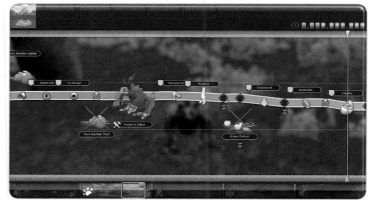

"Development in *Spore* is always this sort of probabilistic production methodology. It's not the traditional way games work."
—CHRIS HECKER, DESIGN & LEAD ENGINEER: PROCEDURAL ANIMATION

Creature Creation

One primary concept of *Spore* is creativity, and nowhere is that creativity more apparent than in the Creature Stage of the game. In this section, we get a glimpse into the process of creating the remarkable creature tools that have become so central to the *Spore* experience, starting with some of the early concept art.

"A bulldozer is something that lets you lift more than you could ever lift with your shovel, and we're starting to get these bulldozers for the mind where you have a creative artist and these tools let them do 10 times more work than they could ever do before."

—Ocean Quigley, Art Director

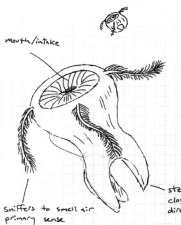

mouth/intake

Floater

environ: Gas giants

move: jet cycle - ingest air to both feed and move. Expell cycle uses lower fingers to ste

eat: Filter Feeder

symetry: trilateral

steering fingers
close during intake cycle
direct expelled air to steer

sniffers to smell air
primary sense

ROLLER

environ: sea floor

move: Slowly slides along ocean floor w/cilia on lower edges. When threatened it rolls into a ball and rolls along surface by squeezing water from the gap

eat: filter, bottom feeder

symetry: bi-lateral

eyes

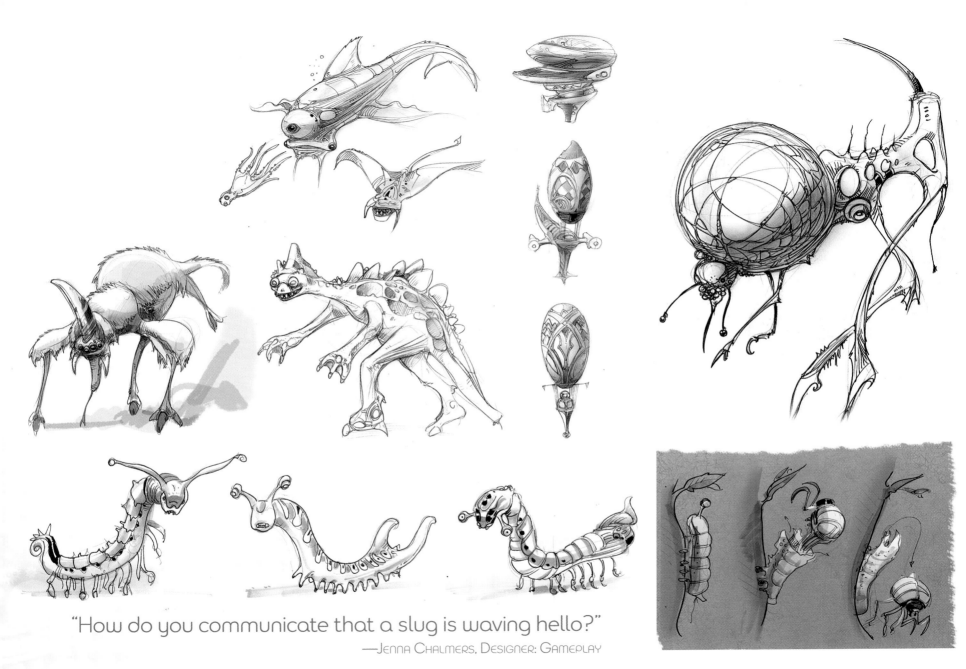

"How do you communicate that a slug is waving hello?"
—Jenna Chalmers, Designer: Gameplay

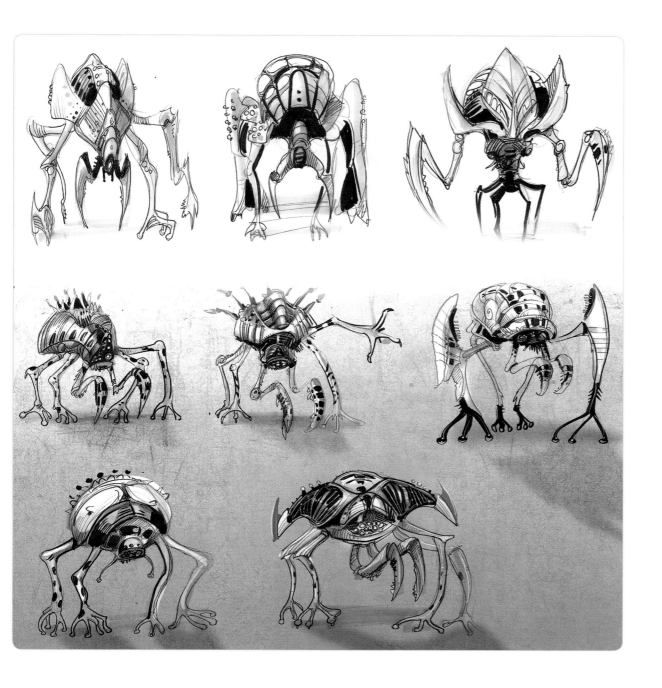
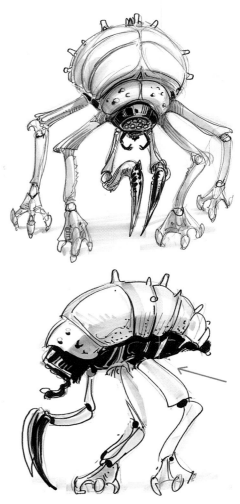

OVERSIZED MAGIC TREES.

SETTLEMENTS

CLASSIC TIM BURTON/DR SEUSS WORLD
INSPIRED BY NIGHTMARE BEFORE CHRISTMAS, BEETLEJUICE OR GRINCH....

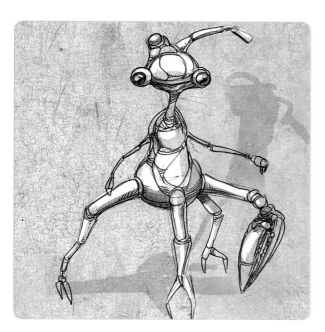

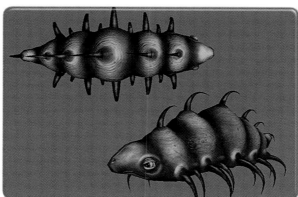

Native from Driftwood Planet

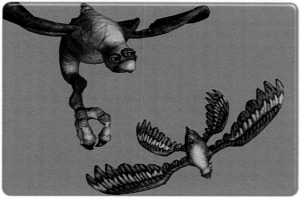

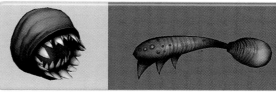

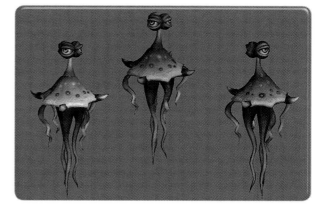

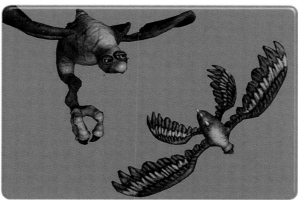

Early Models

The earliest versions of the Creature Creator were very powerful but difficult to use. There were so few rules and limitations that an artist could start piecing bones together in ways that would allow him or her to make anything he or she wanted. The only problem was non-artists were having a lot of trouble making anything that they liked. A lot of times artists on the game would say, "We want more control; take some away from the player so we can make it look better." And the designers would say, "No, it's about complete freedom for the player." So, in the end, we came up with a creator that is a balance of both—creator that promotes lots of creativity and is so easy to use you can jump in and make something awesome in 30 seconds if you want to.

—John Cimino, Animator

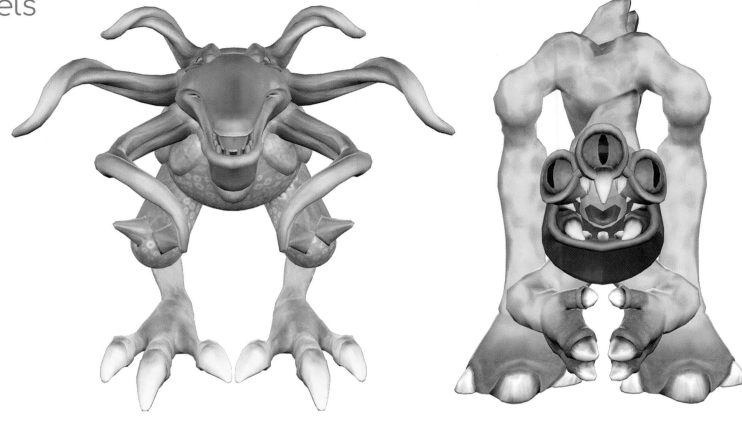

In the early stages of the project, we had the gait system in place as well as complete freedom over what we created in the creator. It was a ton of fun just exploring the creator by making crazy creatures and seeing how they would walk. I remember at one point an intern made a creature that ultimately became somewhat of a legend at Spore. It was called the "Intestisaur" because it looked like some giant mass of intestines all twisted over each other. After he made it we were all wondering what it would look like when it walked around. It was very cool. It really stretched out and moved in a creepy "Intestisaur" type of way. It's always been interesting to see things come to life in ways you did or didn't expect. Just playing with them and seeing how they move. One time I made a creature that looked like a horse. After I built it I had an idea. What if I try to build a rider on top? What will happen? So I did it, and it looked like a limp-wristed corpse riding a horse! Not perfect, but still quite fun. I think the Creature Creator is one of the most entertaining parts of Spore. It's really powerful to be able to make something so quickly that comes to life. Even after years of testing and animating I still enjoy making creatures and hitting the play button.

—JOHN CIMINO, ANIMATOR

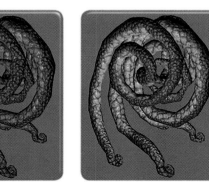

With about a year left in development we finally got around to building ornaments and accessories for the creatures. So you were able to start slapping on different pieces that represented clothing and hats to dress up your creatures and it was a lot

of fun.... Earlier we thought we'd be able to paint on the clothes instead of modeling them.... Some of those early painting tests we did, or I did, still come back to haunt me. They are some of the most embarrassing things I have ever worked on, and people love to bring them up.

—David (Grue) DeBry, Effects and Technical Artist

You get attached very quickly to your characters. Just recently we built some creatures that will ship with the Creature Creator standalone. And they decided to change some of the parts that would go with that, so some of our creatures didn't load up anymore, and I'm like "He's gone!" I had some thumbnails of the creatures, and I'm rebuilding them now, but just for a second I'm like "Aw, Shmookles is gone!"

—Holly Ruark, Artist

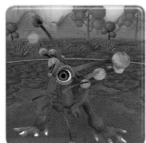

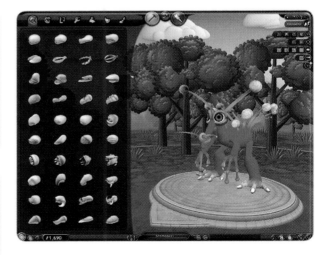

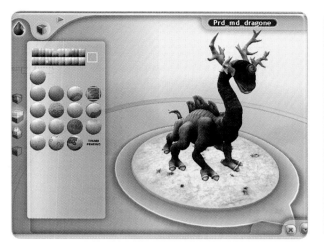

The Creature Creator

The remarkable Creature Creator delights everyone who plays *Spore*, but the creator itself went through many changes as the team struggled to find the right balance of versatility and usability.

Here are some of the first prototype versions of the Creature Creator.

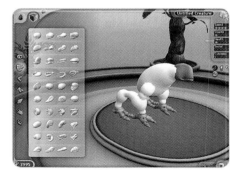

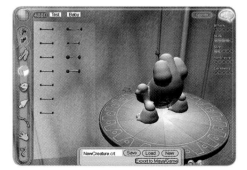

These are early concept mock-ups used to figure out how the Creature Creator would work.

 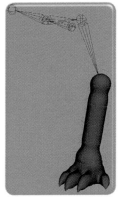 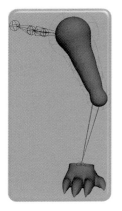 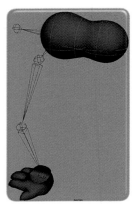 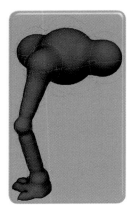 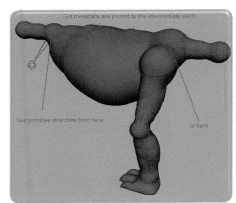

We wanted the Creature game to be about surviving, and evolving your creature to do so. So for us, it was very much about letting players easily go into the creators to develop their creature, and then getting them back into the world to see those various evolutionary adaptations in action.

—MATT POWERS,
PRODUCER: GAMEPLAY

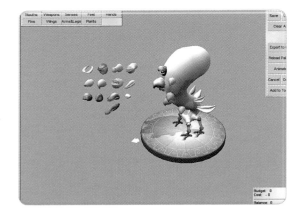

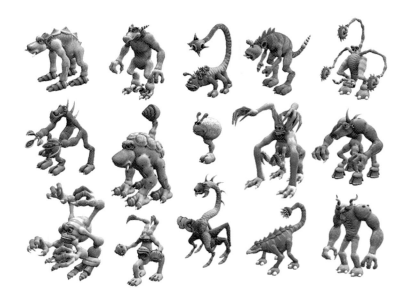

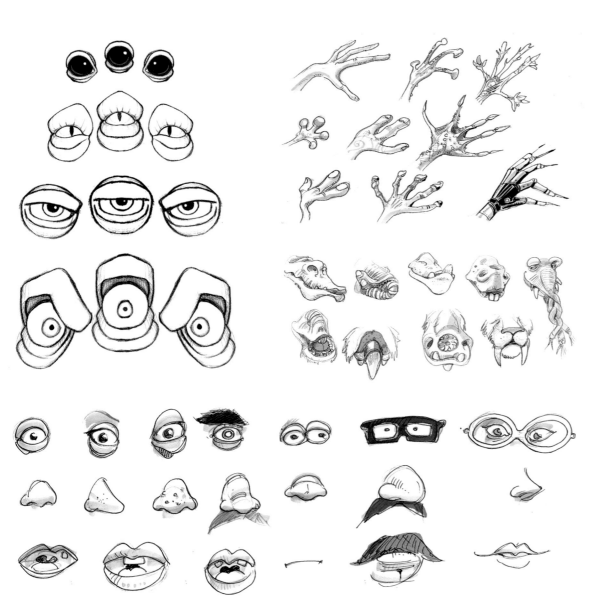

CHEEKS HOIST UPWARDS

BOTTOM TEETH ONLY SHOW

Creature Parts

To make it easy for players to enjoy their creature-creating experience, the *Spore* team created hundreds of sketches and concepts for the parts that could be added to the basic skeleton. Here are some of the early creature parts images.

CHEEKS UP

(A BIT SERPENTINE FROM THE FRONT)

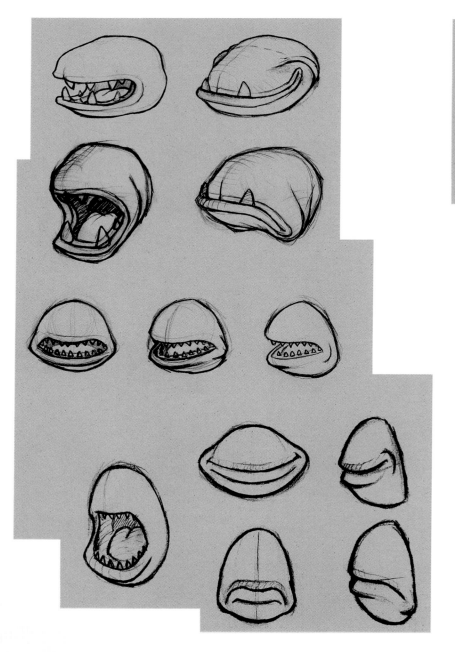

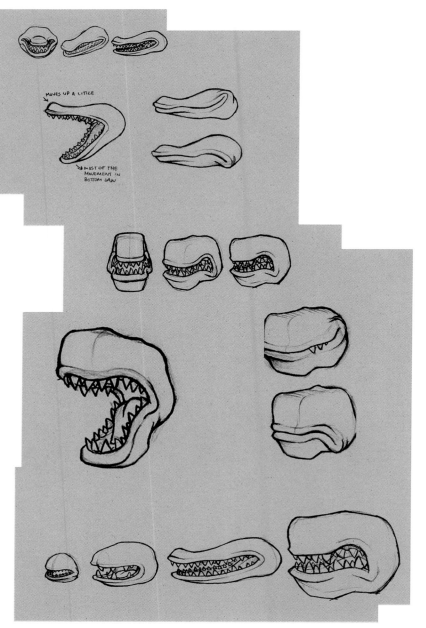

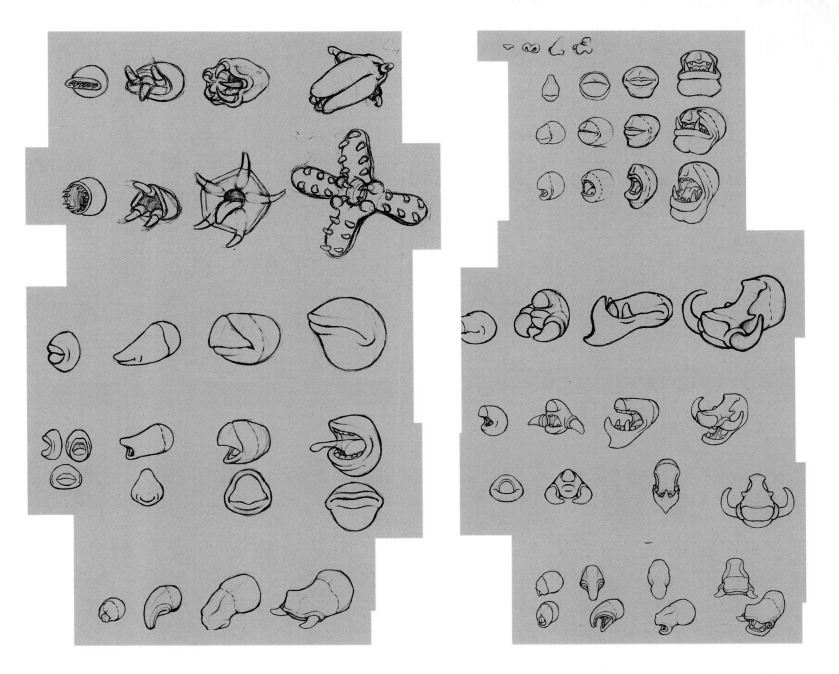

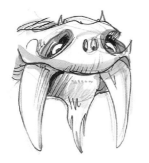

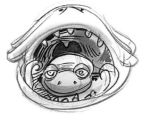

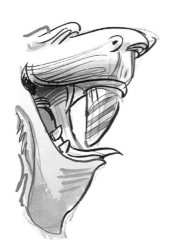

ce_grasper_hand_primate	ce_grasper_hand_primate	ce_grasper_hand_primate	ce_grasper_hand_primate
ce_grasper_claw_insect	ce_grasper_claw_insect	ce_grasper_claw_insect	ce_grasper_claw_insect
ce_grasper_radial	ce_grasper_radial	ce_grasper_radial	ce_grasper_radial
ce_grasper_amphibias	ce_grasper_amphibias	ce_grasper_amphibias	ce_grasper_amphibias
ce_grasper_dino	ce_grasper_dino	ce_grasper_dino	ce_grasper_dino
ce_grasper_paw	ce_grasper_paw	ce_grasper_paw	ce_grasper_paw

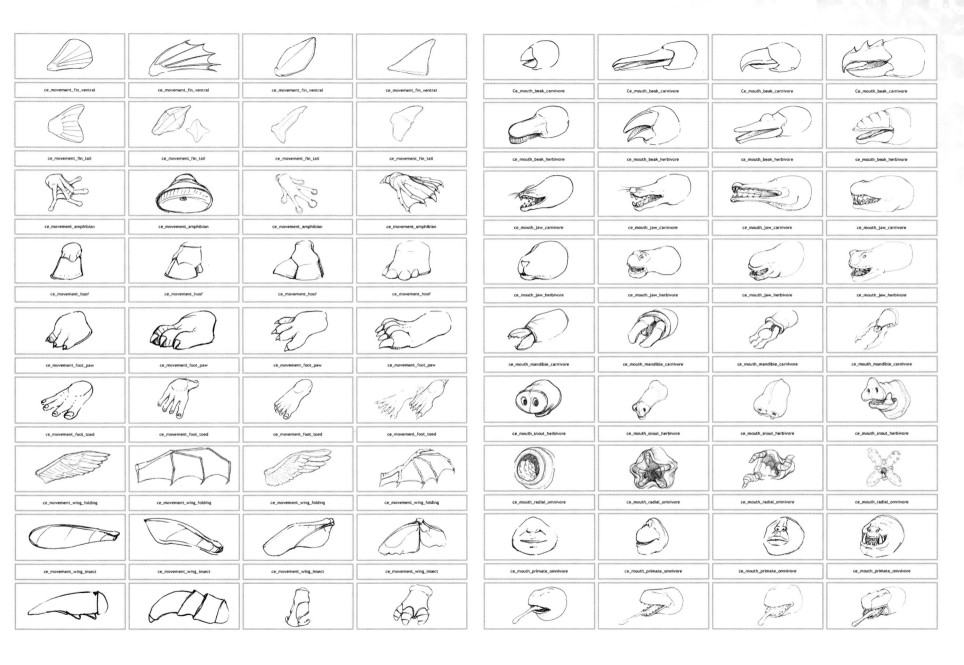

ce_movement_fin_ventral	ce_movement_fin_ventral	ce_movement_fin_ventral	ce_movement_fin_ventral
ce_movement_fin_tail	ce_movement_fin_tail	ce_movement_fin_tail	ce_movement_fin_tail
ce_movement_amphibian	ce_movement_amphibian	ce_movement_amphibian	ce_movement_amphibian
ce_movement_hoof	ce_movement_hoof	ce_movement_hoof	ce_movement_hoof
ce_movement_foot_paw	ce_movement_foot_paw	ce_movement_foot_paw	ce_movement_foot_paw
ce_movement_foot_toed	ce_movement_foot_toed	ce_movement_foot_toed	ce_movement_foot_toed
ce_movement_wing_folding	ce_movement_wing_folding	ce_movement_wing_folding	ce_movement_wing_folding
ce_movement_wing_insect	ce_movement_wing_insect	ce_movement_wing_insect	ce_movement_wing_insect

Ce_mouth_beak_carnivore	Ce_mouth_beak_carnivore	Ce_mouth_beak_carnivore	Ce_mouth_beak_carnivore
ce_mouth_beak_herbivore	ce_mouth_beak_herbivore	ce_mouth_beak_herbivore	ce_mouth_beak_herbivore
ce_mouth_jaw_carnivore	ce_mouth_jaw_carnivore	ce_mouth_jaw_carnivore	ce_mouth_jaw_carnivore
ce_mouth_jaw_herbivore	ce_mouth_jaw_herbivore	ce_mouth_jaw_herbivore	ce_mouth_jaw_herbivore
ce_mouth_mandible_carnivore	ce_mouth_mandible_carnivore	ce_mouth_mandible_carnivore	ce_mouth_mandible_carnivore
ce_mouth_snout_herbivore	ce_mouth_snout_herbivore	ce_mouth_snout_herbivore	ce_mouth_snout_herbivore
ce_mouth_radial_omnivore	ce_mouth_radial_omnivore	ce_mouth_radial_omnivore	ce_mouth_radial_omnivore
ce_mouth_primate_omnivore	ce_mouth_primate_omnivore	ce_mouth_primate_omnivore	ce_mouth_primate_omnivore

Communicating the Creature

One of the main goals of the *Spore* team was to create emotional connection between players and their creations. Here we see a few of the conceptual approaches they used to convey emotion and other cues from the creature to the player.

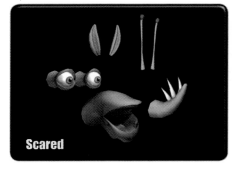
Scared

Neutral

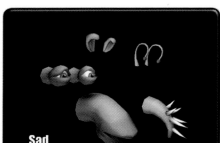
Sad

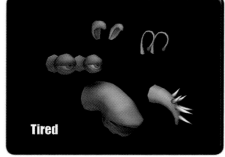
Angry

Tired

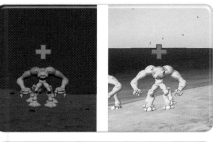

I really don't think having higher res graphics makes me care about a story more. It's more about empathy, connecting with the characters... [it's] more about having the players fully own the characters, because they created them, and that's a different way for us to attach empathy. But I think empathy is really the thing that makes the story come to life for me. I have to care about the characters before the plot or the complex situations. Of course, there are a lot of different paths to get there.

—WILL WRIGHT, *SPORE* VISION & CHIEF DESIGNER

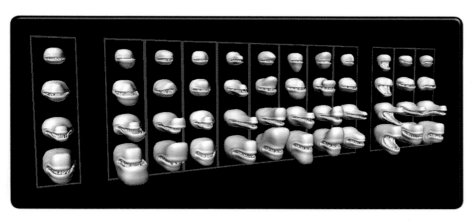

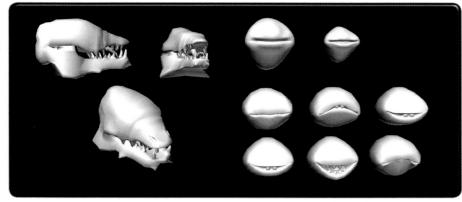

"It's like if you had some clay and built a dog, and it walked around; that's what we're doing."

—BOB KING, DIRECTOR OF ANIMATION

Science vs. Cute

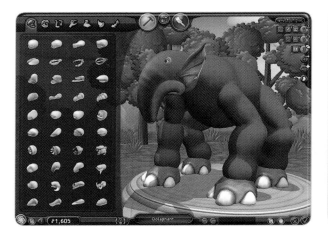

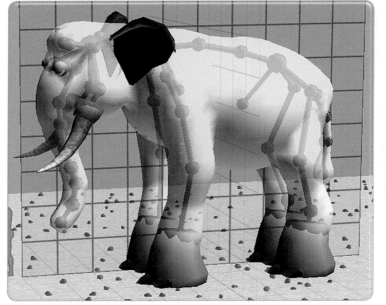

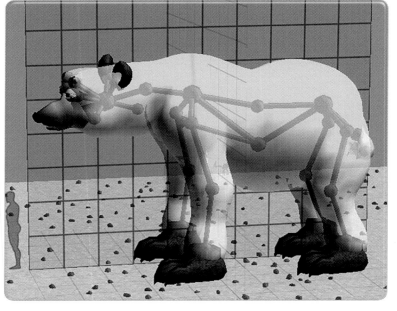

The "cute" team was born, balancing out the project's already well-developed "science" team. Over the next four years, these two teams grew and battled over *Spore*'s heart and sensibility, generating a dynamic balance that ensured *Spore* didn't become another *SimEarth* or *The Jetsons*, but something in between, epic yet accessible.

—Chaim Gingold, Designer: Creators

One of the things we dealt with from the beginning is the fight between—the disagreement, let's say—between the "science" crowd and the "cute" crowd. So we had the people who wanted to make the best-looking, most realistic-looking snake scales possible, and then there's the team who say, "Well, snake scales are cool, but if you're going to go that route then do them cartoony, make them more graphical." And there was a lot of give and take on that for a long time. It took a while to strike a balance.

Ultimately, the nice thing about the creature skins is that there's so many of them, so we can use some of each. There's some in there that are like sequins, that aren't realistic, but are fun. Oh, and there was a small third faction: "science," "cute," and then the "disgusting" crowd. We had a few really disgusting entries for a while, things that looked like bits of other creature's skins, stitched together, with an actual stitching work between each patch, and that was really awful. The balance that was struck in the end between cute and science was, we took a little bit of both, and we pulled them both in a little bit so we don't have any really really sciency stuff, and don't have any really really graphical stuff. And the balance was struck partially because both crowds needed to work and play together, and also because the controlling factor is the animations. If you have an animation system that made really realistic movements then you can use a more realistic texture, and likewise if you have more cartoony movement we can do that. The animation is really impressive, but it doesn't go all the way in both areas, so the balance was struck.

—David (Grue) DeBry, Effects and Technical Artist

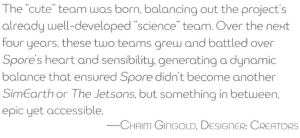

The decision to incorporate the character design aesthetic of an animator marked a turning point in the visual sensibility of the project. The genetic building blocks of *Spore's* life forms, the creature parts, adopted the appeal and personality of John Cimino's creature designs. And imagining how Pixar might visually treat a film about bacteria, we put eyes on our single-celled organisms. Our planets transformed into expansive landscapes but retained a toylike sensibility. We made the galaxy more colorful. The entire team became vigilant, seeking opportunities to inject charm and wit into the project, producing the dry goofball humor that characterizes Maxis games.

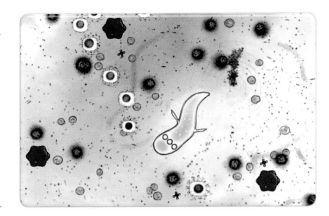

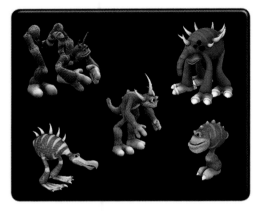

Not that there was a mad rush for cartoony style, humor, and anthropomorphism. Each art review and design meeting had the potential to shift the balance of power between the "cute" and "science" teams, which is how we caricatured the opposed design sensibilities and their proponents. *Spore's* style was a compromise worked out over many years between a scientific, realistic, and weighty aesthetic, and something popular, appealing, and full of personality.

—Chaim Gingold, Designer: Creators

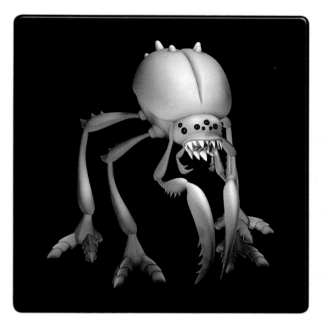

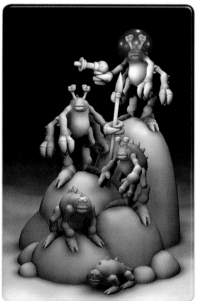

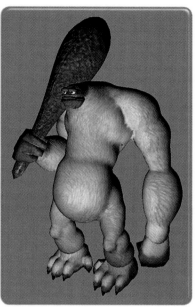

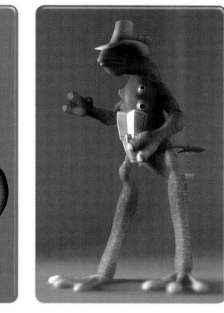

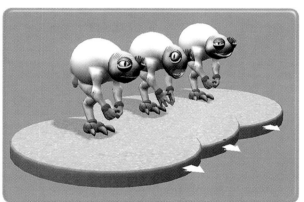

The idea of science vs. cute brings up an interesting balance, because you're dealing with a thing that overtly seems fairly scientific. We're dealing with universe-level time scales: We're dealing with evolution, we're dealing with astronomy, sociology. But at the same time we are dealing with the innate playfulness of the players, and of this world. We are dealing with a caricature of the universe—kind of a vast simplification—but the main thing is that we want the player to approach it playfully. And that's where, at some levels of the game we want them to feel the awe and inspiration of science, and at other levels we want players to be encouraged to do just funny, goofy, silly things, and to laugh out loud at what they have done. So we're always trying to strike a balance, at every level, between these two things—really, almost between reality and play.

—Will Wright, Spore Vision & Chief Designer

Procedural Animation

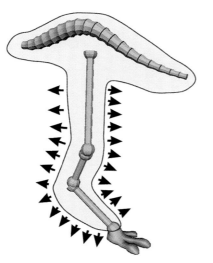

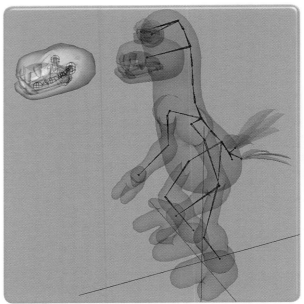

"We had to create a system where the animation system has to figure out how to animate it when it doesn't know the bone structure ahead of time."

—CHRIS HECKER, DESIGN & LEAD ENGINEER: PROCEDURAL ANIMATION

A Mad Lib analogy is probably the best way to describe our animation system. See, in a normal animation system, each bone of the character of James Bond has a number, right? And when you select a bone in Maya, like you click on his hand, which let's say is Bone 42, you then take Bone 42 and you move it and you record a key frame. And Bone 42 is at XYZ whatever coordinates. But we have to work totally differently. We have this query system that says, "I want to look for hands." Not Bone 42, because Bone 42 might be the back on some other creature, right? So you write this query which says, "What am I trying to select? I'm trying to select a hand." Okay, but what if you have three hands on the right-hand side? Do you want all of them? Do you want the front-most one? Do you want the animation to be able to vary, using this Variants system, saying that the gameplay can pick which one the animation plays back on, and the others play this kind of default thing? So you have to describe all that to the system. And then, you can't just move to XYZ coordinates. You have to say, "I'm trying to move it relative to this hand or relative to the ground or relative to that target, or just in space around the creature.

—Chris Hecker, Design & Lead Engineer: Procedural Animation

There was so much unscripted and unplanned humor that came out of the AI. I remember we were in one of our playthrough meetings, in the middle of the process, and trying to get a creature to pick fruit from a tree. This doesn't sound tremendously hard, but if you think about what we're doing with creature physiologies and procedural animation, it's actually a very difficult concept. We came up with a system where the creature would pick up a stick (if he was too short and couldn't reach the fruit) and hit the base of the tree. This would cause the fruit to fall and the creature could then get it. We tested this concept on one of the herbivores so we would be sure that he would eat the fruit. During this time, the NPCs creatures are doing their thing and are running around the field in the background. We got into a recurring behavior where the creature would hit the tree and nothing would happen, as there was a random element to the frequency of when the fruit would fall. After 3–4 minutes of this, finally the creature hits the tree, the fruit falls and the engine runs a success animation. The creature begins celebrating, waving his arms and shouting his version of "Hurrah!" As he is celebrating, an NPC creature came out of nowhere and ate the fruit and left! It was completely unplanned, but it was very funny. We didn't script that behavior, it just played out that way. The NPC creature was hungry, and some food just happened to fall in its radius of action. Before we got to the main creature eating it, the NPC creature came in and ate it.

—Bob King, Director of Animation

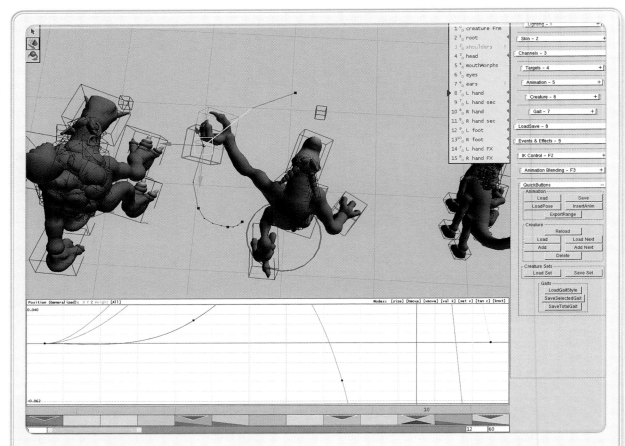

Working as an animator on *Spore* can definitely try your patience. You're animating for creatures that you have never seen before so you have to be a little willing to compromise or the game simply won't work. When I first started, my main goal was to make animation files that were super polished, specific, and looked awesome. When you try that, you quickly realize that something that's really subtle and pretty on one guy will end up looking horrible on everybody else. After you make it and load in another little creature to test it on, your reaction is usually something along the line of, "Argh!" It's always funny to watch Bob, the animation director, get frustrated at the lack of control over the creatures. He's an old-school animator. If he had his choice, he would make *Spore* as a stop motion animation with nothing but clay and a camera made in 1972. It's a big challenge for animators because were normally pretty anal and dislike lack of control. In *Spore*, the goal wasn't perfection but massive generalization.

—John Cimino, Animator

Half of animation is character design, which we don't have control over. So by design we don't have very real distinct animation. So if people want to build a leopard, it's not going to move accurately, it is all cartoony and bouncy ... [or] it looks awful and doesn't move right, and you can hear the bones and tendons snapping. We went for another style of more fun animation, which worked out well, even though it was spawned from the limitations of this stuff.

—Bob King, Director of Animation

"When you fail,
make sure you fail funny."

—Chris Hecker, Design & Lead Engineer:
Procedural Animation
quoting Will Wright

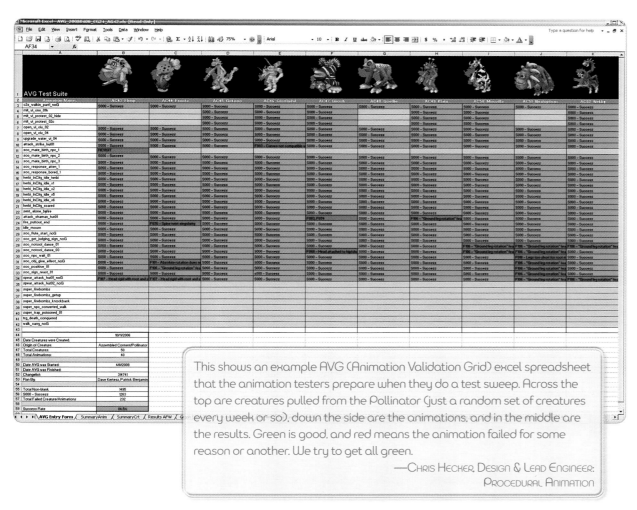

This shows an example AVG (Animation Validation Grid) excel spreadsheet that the animation testers prepare when they do a test sweep. Across the top are creatures pulled from the Pollinator (just a random set of creatures every week or so), down the side are the animations, and in the middle are the results. Green is good, and red means the animation failed for some reason or another. We try to get all green.

—Chris Hecker, Design & Lead Engineer: Procedural Animation

"You don't want the majority of people to even notice that anything magical is going on."

—Chris Hecker, Design & Lead Engineer: Procedural Animation

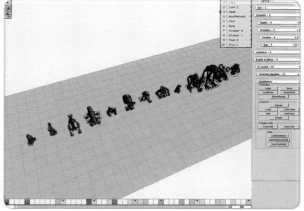

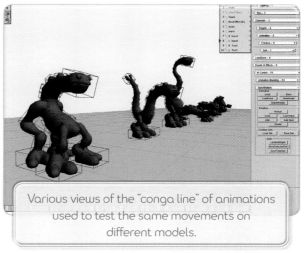

Various views of the "conga line" of animations used to test the same movements on different models.

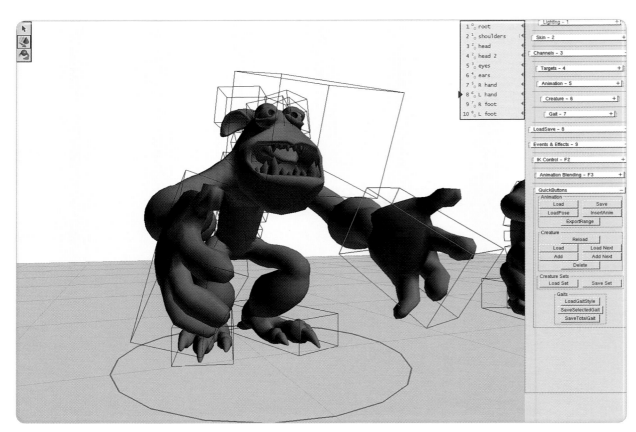

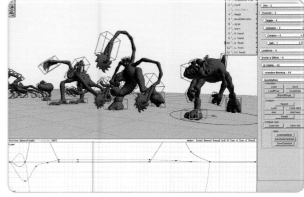

The first time seeing a creature you built in the game walk around using the animation system we thought of—that's just amazing.... We built the creature creator system from scratch, which works in sync with the animation tool we built from scratch, and they just blend together. Any creature you make will run the animation you made for a happy dance or whatever. It's just amazing.

—Bob King, Director of Animation

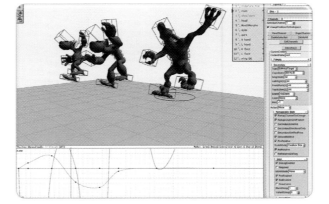

Testers at work, using the Spasm system to check animations across multiple models.

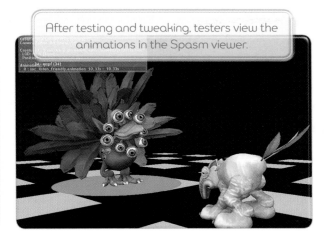

After testing and tweaking, testers view the animations in the Spasm viewer.

The Challenge of Hands

When animating, the biggest problem we've had with generalizing across a large group of creatures usually comes from the arms. The feet generalize pretty well because they are always planted on the ground and the head works fine because it's normally just nodding up and down and turning in place. The arms, however, are a bit of a challenge. The player can arrange them in so many different ways that will break an animation that we really had to think about everything we did when it came to animating hand gestures.

—John Cimino, Animator

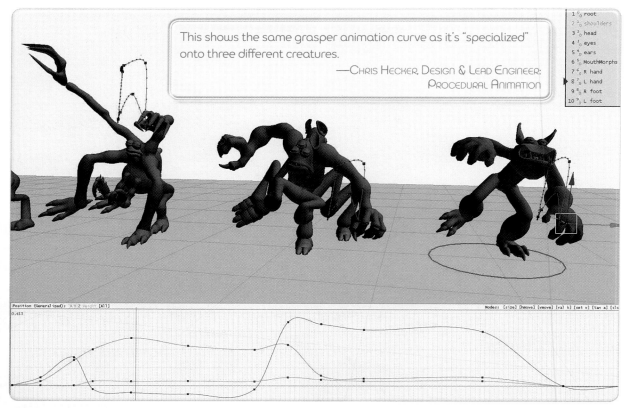

This shows the same grasper animation curve as it's "specialized" onto three different creatures.

—Chris Hecker, Design & Lead Engineer:
Procedural Animation

1	root
2	shoulders
3	head
4	eyes
5	ears
6	MouthMorphs
7	R hand
8	L hand
9	R foot
10	L foot

Position (Generalized): X Y Z Height [All]   Modes: [size] [hmove] [vmove] [val k] [set v] [tan a] [slc

0.413

We have great bugs. I mean, games always have great bugs, but when you have this crazy procedural animation system and the player can do anything, there are examples about how the animation system doesn't really understand everything about the creature, like the example of the clapping animation where the creature's head ended up between the hands, and the guy kept smacking himself in the head. Like if you were doing that animation at Pixar, you'd know to dodge down before you did it, but the animation system doesn't try to collision-detect the entire creature because it's too slow.

It's like this endless battle against user creativity, in some sense. But the payoff is huge. You go in the creator and you stick an arm on your guy and he rears back and looks at his arm and you go, "Whoa! That guy just came to life!" But it's one of those things. If we do a great job on the animation system, people won't notice it anymore.

—Chris Hecker, Design & Lead Engineer:
Procedural Animation

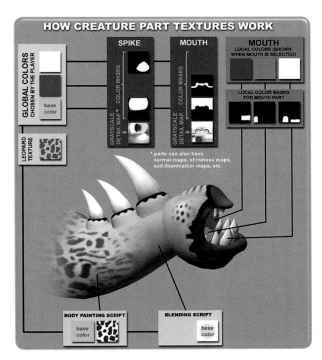

HOW CREATURE PART TEXTURES WORK

GLOBAL COLORS CHOSEN BY THE PLAYER

base color

LEOPARD TEXTURE

SPIKE
GRAYSCALE DETAIL MAP * · COLOR MASKS

MOUTH
GRAYSCALE DETAIL MAP * · COLOR MASKS

MOUTH
LOCAL COLORS (SHOWN WHEN MOUTH IS SELECTED)

LOCAL COLOR MASKS FOR MOUTH PART

* parts can also have
normal maps, shininess maps,
self-illumination maps, etc.

BODY PAINTING SCRIPT
base color

BLENDING SCRIPT
base color

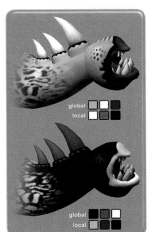

global
local

global
local

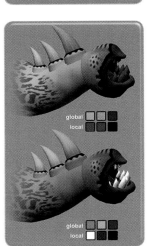

global
local

global
local

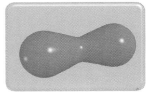 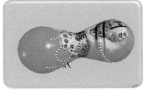 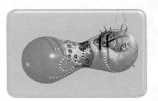

 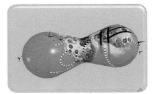 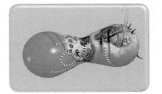

  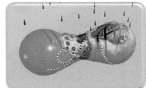

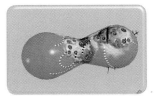 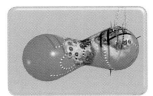 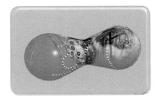

Procedural Texture Mapping

Spore is a weird game in that all the systems to make the stuff are procedural, so instead of making art and sticking it in the game, I've got to make systems that make things that get them in the game.

So what we've got to do is analyze the model, break it down into elements upon which we can make decisions, and then run these little texture script programs that can clamber over the creature, painting it as they go.

In most games, the art director says, "This is what I want it to look like," and the artists build it. In *Spore*, instead of art-directing artists, which is the usual thing, I'm art-directing engineers and trying to come up with systems that will get us the aesthetic we want.

—OCEAN QUIGLEY, ART DIRECTOR

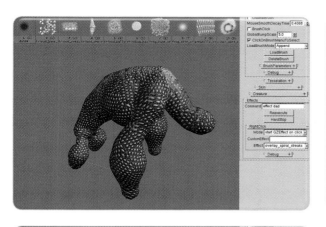

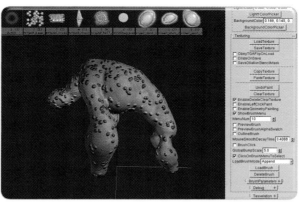

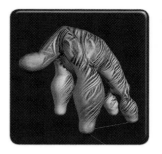

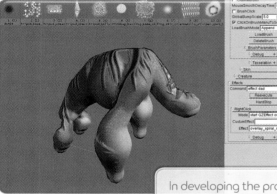

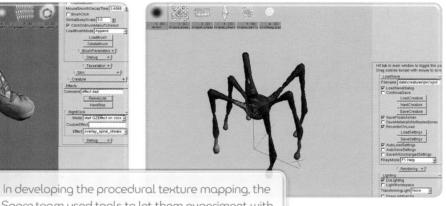

In developing the procedural texture mapping, the *Spore* team used tools to let them experiment with all the possible options.

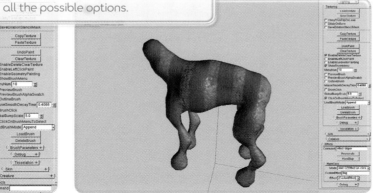

We're expecting that players are going to want and expect results that are professional quality. But the players aren't artists and we haven't anticipated all the possible things they might want to do. So we made systems for texturing creatures that have scripts that drop agents, these little particles that are able to clamber about the skin and paint on it.

For example, there's a particle that says, "I'm the kind of particle that paints stripes down the back of the spine." It identifies spines and paints stripes down them. Another might put spots on legs. Essentially we had to write little programs to figure out how to texture creatures.

It's kind of strange, because most of my texture artists are used to working in Photoshop and Maya, but for *Spore* we had to teach these texture artists how to program. Most of the content in *Spore* is like that—instead of building stuff that comes canned and goes into the game, we had to make these dynamic systems that are able to take parts, reconnect them in various ways, decimate* them, bake** them, and get them into the game.

—Ocean Quigley, Art Director

*decimate—to reduce the triangle count so that it's low-poly enough to render in quantity

**bake—to take the model made out of lots of different parts with different textures and make a single textured, skinned model out of it, so it can be handled as a single element

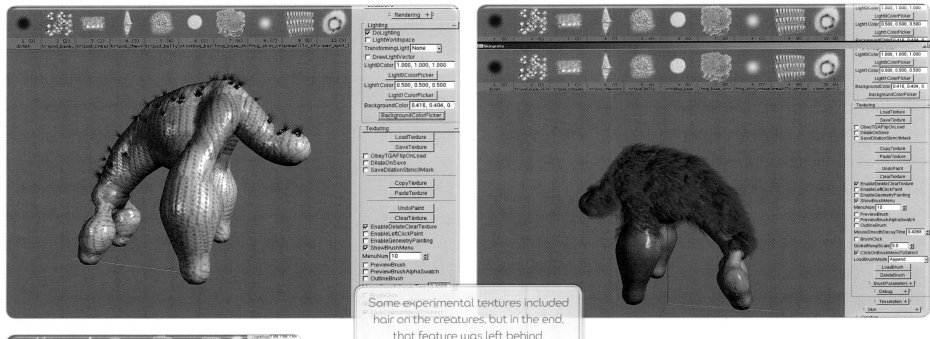

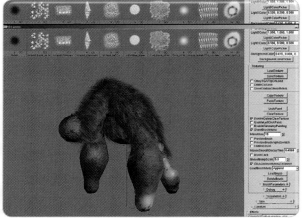

Some experimental textures included hair on the creatures, but in the end, that feature was left behind.

Almost all textures in games these days go through Photoshop, where every pixel is touched, and we don't have that luxury. So we had to create a system that could run online, on the user's machine. So we use all these things that no real texture artists would even imagine. For example, in a "real" game, you're doing James Bond and you make the mesh, and you have to unwrap the mesh into a 2-D sheet, so you can texture map it. It's like butterflying a chicken, right? And it's kind of a point of pride among texture artists how well they can do that—how little distortion they can achieve, and whether they've got the right amount of texture density in various areas—the triangles are big enough in texture space, or whatever, and they're not wasting space and it's all packed together. And we do an incredibly bad job of that, but we do it in 10 milliseconds, whereas a normal texture artist might take four or five hours to do that. I mean, 10 milliseconds goes into four or five hours, like a million times, right? So we're a million times faster, but we can't be a million times worse. We're probably six or eight times worse and a million times faster. So hey! So Ocean once said about the texture charter that I wrote, "I'd fire an artist that did a texture that bad—but, 10 milliseconds!"

—Chris Hecker, Design & Lead Engineer: Procedural Animation

When I joined the project, my first major rethink, coming from a film background, was going from a 24-hour render per frame to less than a second render per frame. And some of my original creature skins were detailed work and took several seconds to render, which I thought was phenomenal. And then I was told I was taking too long! So that was my own personal dilemma.

—David (Grue) DeBry, Effects and Technical Artist

These show the texture "charting," with a 3-D view of a frog-shaped creature, and the texture map. You can see what I was saying about the chart being pretty hard to parse visually, but you can see chunks of the frog in there, and the software handles painting into the texture and deals with the seams.

—Chris Hecker, Design & Lead Engineer: Procedural Animation

The art director still has very strong control over the full look of the game and are doing a great job.... But we know here—and it's one of the fun and scary things of working on *Spore*—is that whatever we try and do, once someone gets the game on their computer, we have to hope it holds up. They are going to basically exploit every possible angle of this, and that's super cool, but it's super cool and also a little scary.

—David (Grue) DeBry, Effects and Technical Artist

Creator Fun

We'll leave you with a few more fun images from the *Spore* Team.

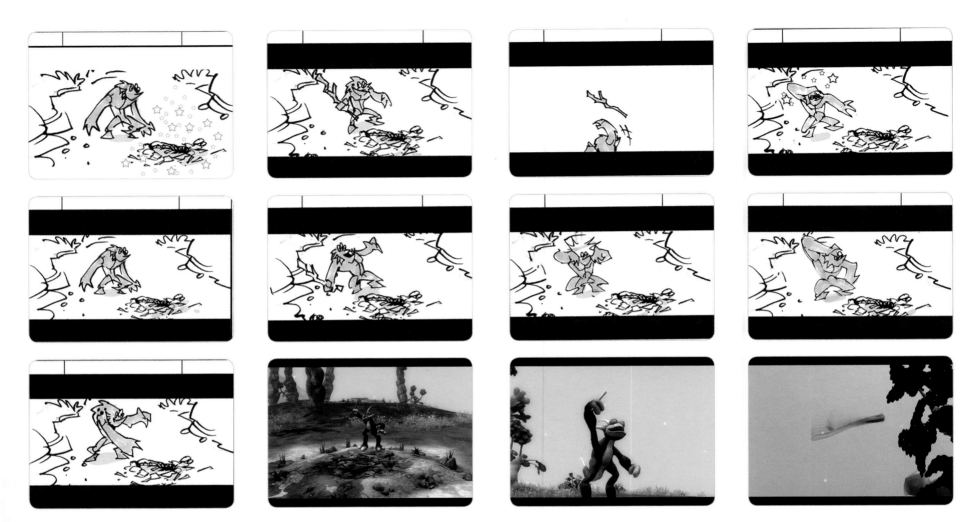

These storyboards were used to visualize the cutscene when the creature reaches the Tribal Stage. In a humorous homage to the movie *2001: A Space Odyssey*, the creature discovers the power of tools by bonking himself over the head with a stick. With tools, comes the advent of the tribe.

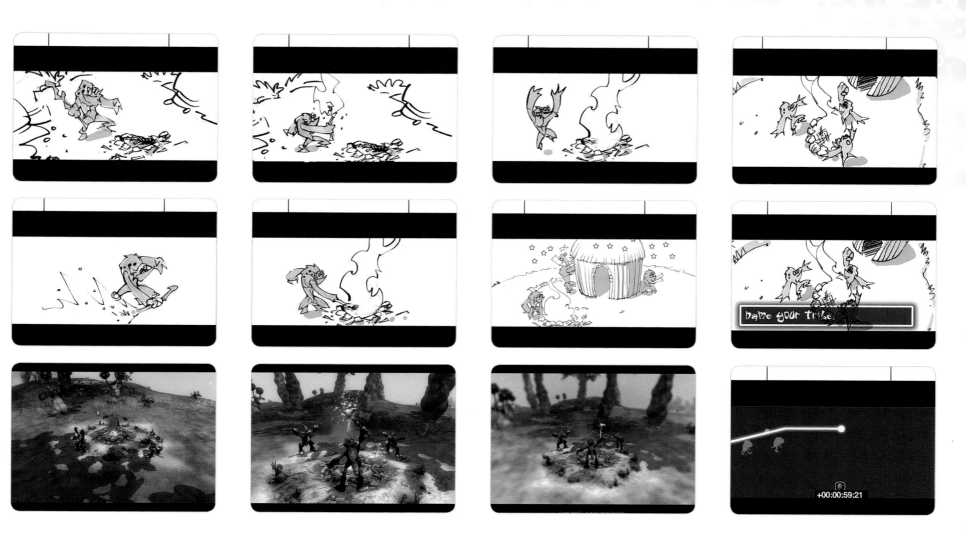

3 tribe
stage

In all the game levels, we were looking to not only have an interesting game with interesting rules and interesting mechanics, but also add elements of charm and humor to each one of the stages. And those entertaining characteristics needed to appropriately reflect the stage of evolution we set the player in.... So in the Creature game, the creatures need to carry on in a more creature- or animal-like way. In Tribe game, the player is controlling sentient beings that should have more sophisticated behaviors. So it's a more "evolved" type of charm and humor we are looking for.

Hopefully in Tribe game, what we walk away with is not only a play experience that has interesting rules, interesting mechanics, and interesting objectives in terms of how you unify the tribes, but also a feeling that this creature that I have evolved from my Creature game now looks advanced and intelligent, as far as a member of a tribal society would look. And it's humorous; it's funny; it's entertaining.... We see a lot of people spinning the camera around to watch their tribe members.... So for us, it's not only about being functional and compelling gameplay-wise; at the end of the day, it also needs to be fun to watch.

—Matt Powers, Producer: Gameplay

The Tribe Concept

One challenge for us in this game is managing depth against complexity. In the Tribe game, we were always looking for opportunities to add depth but were mindful of the complexity it would bring. We didn't want these game experiences to feel simple, but we wanted them to feel accessible. So we would look at new propositions and say, "This would be really cool, but for the play experience, how complex is it?"

—MATT POWERS, PRODUCER: GAMEPLAY

"I think empathy is really the thing that makes the story come to life for me. I have to care about the characters before the plot or the complex situations."

—WILL WRIGHT, SPORE VISION & CHIEF DESIGNER

Storyboards describe the evolution of the Tribe Stage.

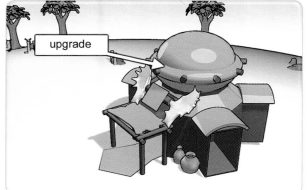

upgrade

Early concepts of the Tribe Stage

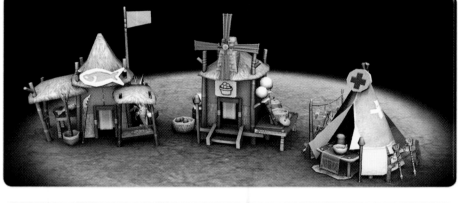

Early challenges in placing the tribal village

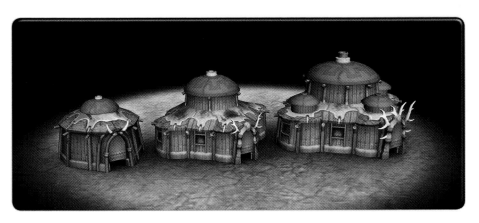

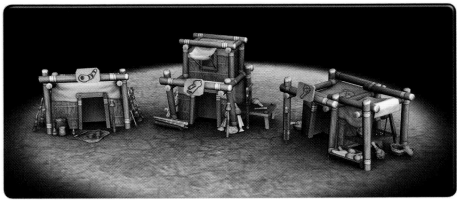

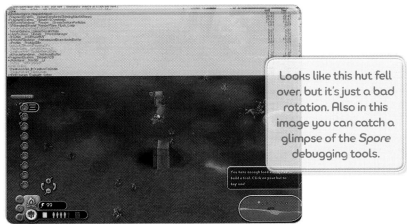

Looks like this hut fell over, but it's just a bad rotation. Also in this image you can catch a glimpse of the *Spore* debugging tools.

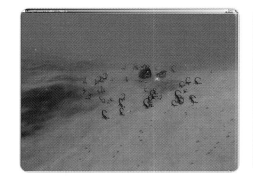

Early in development, a recurring bug often put tribal villages underwater—giving a hint of what the lost underwater level could have resembled.

Creating a mask for the tribe's village

 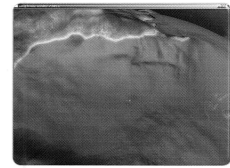

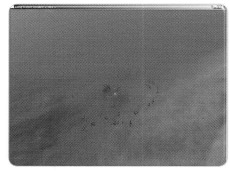 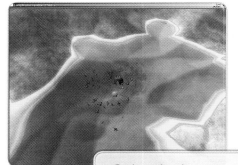

Early in development, tribal villages and cities could be underwater. Underwater creatures and gameplay were taken out of the game, however.

You have made the Blue Village your allies!

Players sometimes want to create a nonaggressive character, and that is possible, although we've heard from people who like to go the nonaggressive path say that at some point they decided to exact revenge on a particular species for any number of reasons. In so doing, they kind of start to write a new fiction for themselves. That's part of the charm. You can evolve your fiction as you evolve your creature; it's not binary. You don't have to go completely combative or social. You can navigate the parts of that spectrum as you wish, and I think that's one of the nice parts of this game.

—Matt Powers, Producer: Gameplay

Another interesting challenge we had in Tribe was that because we were bringing in creatures from other people's games, people had a difficulty distinguishing their own tribe from wild creatures. Early on, we thought that even though we lock physical evolution at the end of the Creature Stage, people might want to do things like make them stand more upright or change their posture to make them look more intelligent, but it turned out to be impossible to do in code in an attractive way, and it wasn't really desirable anyway because we didn't want to mess with people's creations. You might have spent hours making it just right and then we came along and ruined it for you. Best just to leave well enough alone.

—Alex Hutchinson, Lead Designer: Gameplay

Early Concept Sketches

Huts

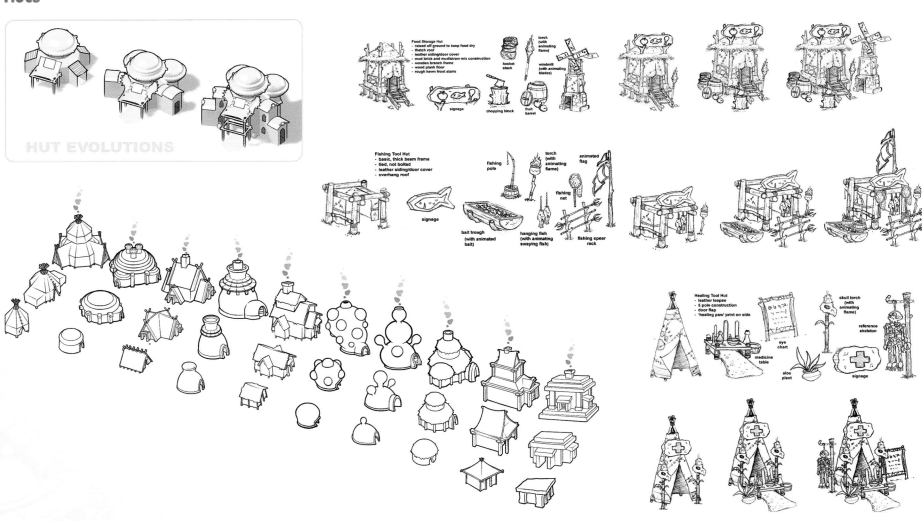

HUT EVOLUTIONS

Food Storage Hut
- raised off ground to keep food dry
- thatch roof
- leather siding/door cover
- mud brick and mud/straw mix construction
- wooden branch frame
- wood plank floor
- rough hewn front stairs

signage

basket stack

chopping block

fruit barrel

torch (with animating flame)

windmill (with animating blades)

Fishing Tool Hut
- basic, thick beam frame
- tied, not bolted
- leather siding/door cover
- overhang roof

fishing pole

torch (with animating flame)

animated flag

fishing net

signage

bait trough (with animated bait)

hanging fish (with animating swaying fish)

fishing spear rack

Healing Tool Hut
- leather teepee
- 5 pole construction
- door flap
- 'healing paw' print on side

eye chart

skull torch (with animating flame)

reference skeleton

medicine table

aloe plant

signage

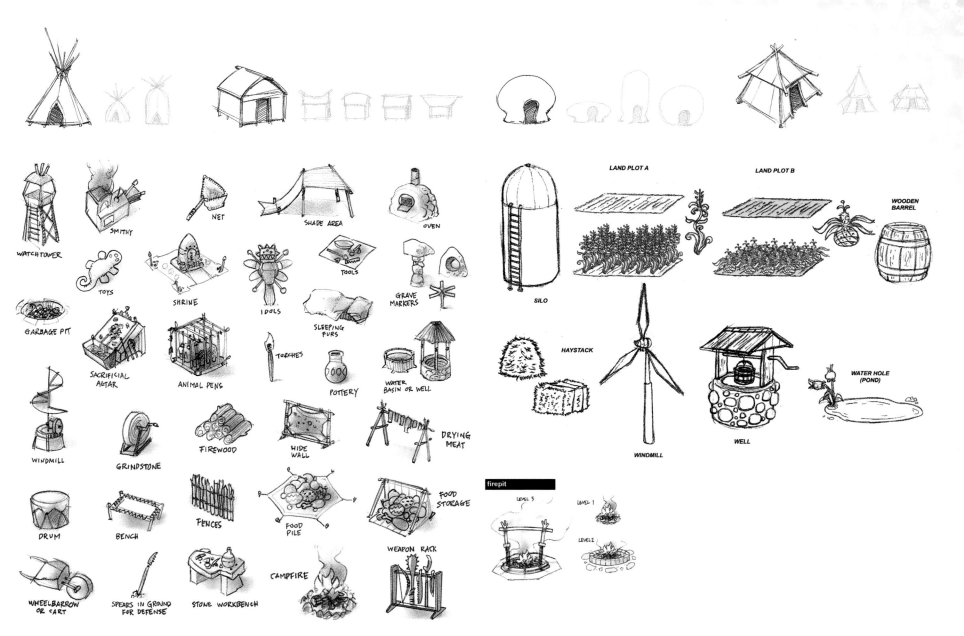

WATCHTOWER

SMITHY

NET

SHADE AREA

OVEN

TOYS

SHRINE

IDOLS

TOOLS

GRAVE MARKERS

GARBAGE PIT

SACRIFICIAL ALTAR

ANIMAL PENS

SLEEPING FURS

TORCHES

POTTERY

WATER BASIN OR WELL

WINDMILL

GRINDSTONE

FIREWOOD

HIDE WALL

DRYING MEAT

DRUM

BENCH

FENCES

FOOD PILE

FOOD STORAGE

WHEELBARROW OR CART

SPEARS IN GROUND FOR DEFENSE

STONE WORKBENCH

CAMPFIRE

WEAPON RACK

SILO

LAND PLOT A

LAND PLOT B

WOODEN BARREL

HAYSTACK

WINDMILL

WELL

WATER HOLE (POND)

firepit

LEVEL 3

LEVEL 1

LEVEL 2

Tools

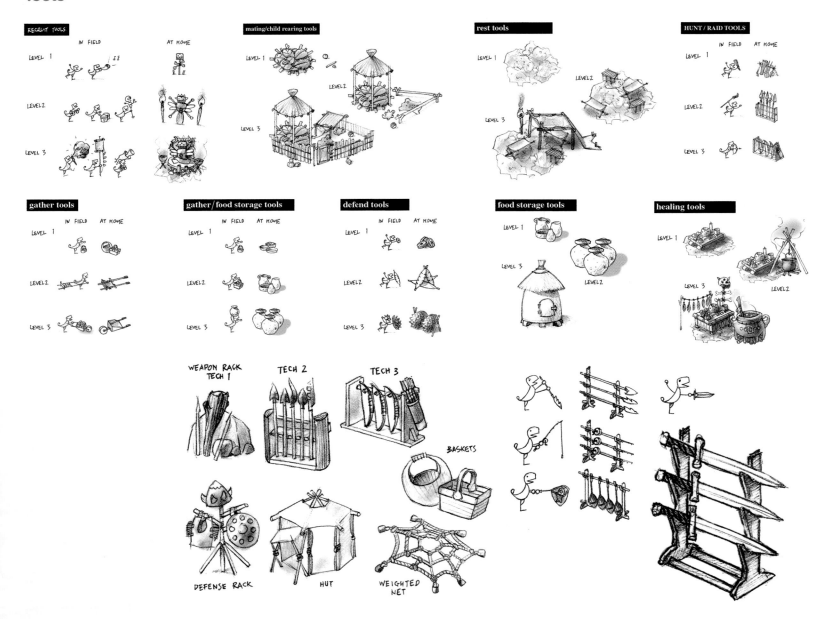

RECRUIT TOOLS

IN FIELD   AT HOME

LEVEL 1

LEVEL2

LEVEL 3

mating/child rearing tools

LEVEL 1

LEVEL2

LEVEL 3

rest tools

LEVEL 1

LEVEL2

LEVEL 3

HUNT / RAID TOOLS

IN FIELD   AT HOME

LEVEL 1

LEVEL2

LEVEL 3

gather tools

IN FIELD   AT HOME

LEVEL 1

LEVEL2

LEVEL 3

gather/food storage tools

IN FIELD   AT HOME

LEVEL 1

LEVEL2

LEVEL 3

defend tools

IN FIELD   AT HOME

LEVEL 1

LEVEL2

LEVEL 3

food storage tools

LEVEL 1

LEVEL 3

LEVEL2

healing tools

LEVEL 1

LEVEL 3

LEVEL2

WEAPON RACK TECH 1

TECH 2

TECH 3

BASKETS

DEFENSE RACK

HUT

WEIGHTED NET

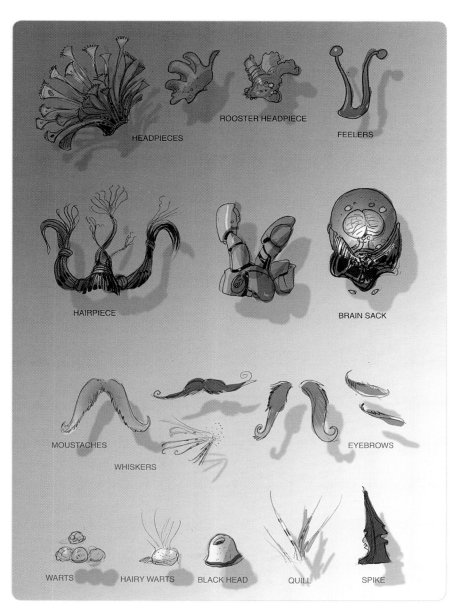

HEADPIECES

ROOSTER HEADPIECE

FEELERS

HAIRPIECE

BRAIN SACK

MOUSTACHES

WHISKERS

EYEBROWS

WARTS

HAIRY WARTS

BLACK HEAD

QUILL

SPIKE

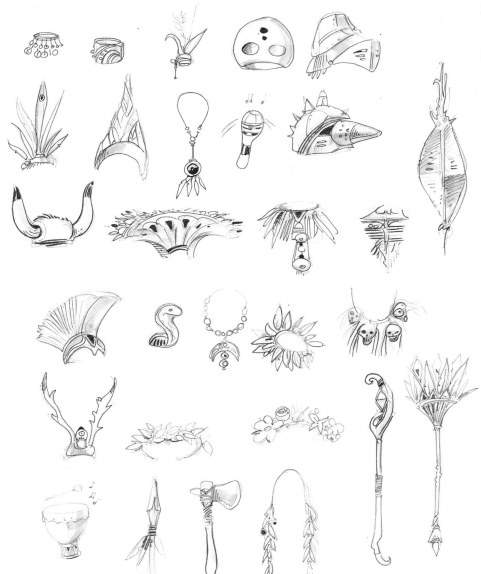

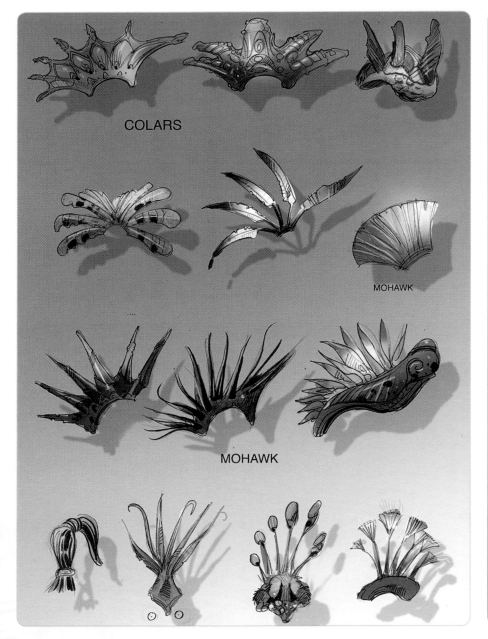

COLARS

MOHAWK

MOHAWK

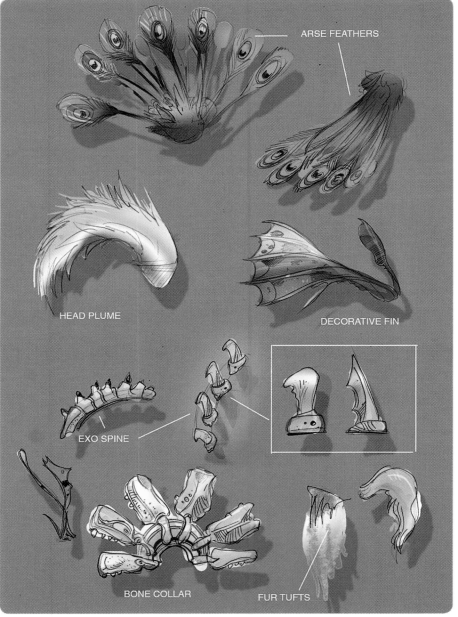

ARSE FEATHERS

HEAD PLUME

DECORATIVE FIN

EXO SPINE

BONE COLLAR

FUR TUFTS

Tribe Buildings, Tools, and Accessories

The essence of the Tribe game is in using the buildings, tools, and accessories to help your tribe become the conqueror or the friend to all other tribes. Here's a look at some of the development work that went into making those elements.

The basic creature abilities are far less relevant in the Tribe game. Tribe is about the tools and using the tools.
—Alex Hutchinson, Lead Designer: Gameplay

In Tribe game, the biggest animation generalization challenge came with creatures using tools. It's one thing to animate a bunch of creatures with arms swinging a club. But what if the player decides not to give him any hands? In those cases we had to branch the animation. We made one for the guys with hands, and then another for the guys without. For the grasperless creatures we'd put the club in the mouth and had them swing their heads around. That's probably not the most effective way to attack with a club, but it looked kind of funny and we really didn't want to limit the players by telling them they had to have hands to play Tribe game. Sometimes in *Spore* if things are funny they get a free pass.

—John Cimino, Animator

To me, the game is quite comical. You'll have one tribe deciding to socialize with you and then you'll have other tribe deciding to conquer you with violence. So in certain situations you'll have creatures come over and give you a gift while another group pays you a visit armed with axes and spears. The tribe that was trying to give you a gift will get upset and attack them. Then you have chaos. Three tribes all attacking each other in a big brawl. Then I'm always like, "What's going on!" It's funny.

—John Cimino, Animator

One problem we had on Tribe was real-world gameplay fiction vs. expectations. Real-world fiction states that only one species should become intelligent and this is how Will originally envisioned it. On the gameplay side though, when everyone looks like you, players start thinking, "Why can't I control this guy who looks just like me?" And also, if you have just one species, then all the tribes are identical from a tuning perspective—then the only strategy is gaining superior numbers. So we eventually switched it so other tribes were different species, but the most important reason to change it in my opinion is that *Spore* is a game that celebrates content and we should use every excuse to show the player more unique creations.

—Alex Hutchinson, Lead Designer: Gameplay

Another global ongoing *Spore* argument was how challenging to make it. If you are making storytelling software or making a toy, then it shouldn't be hard. But every time you present that concept to gamers, too often they tend to respond negatively. Most game players relish challenge and complicated strategies and controls, but we had to hit something that was much easier to use and much simpler to play than most strategy games. Our aim was to make a game that made people feel creative, and by people I don't just mean gamers, I mean your average person on the street.

That's a very important issue for me, especially when we're talking about the gameplay. In some ways our goals and philosophy of design are hamstringing us at every step, taking on lots of problems, but interesting ones. In the Tribe game, you have to bridge between being sort of a sedentary nomadic caveman to the growth of technology. It's more about telling a story than building a challenge, which again is a very unusual way to break down a game—showing you your creations in a new setting and presenting new challenges to overcome, but still keeping it loose and light.
—Alex Hutchinson, Lead Designer: Gameplay

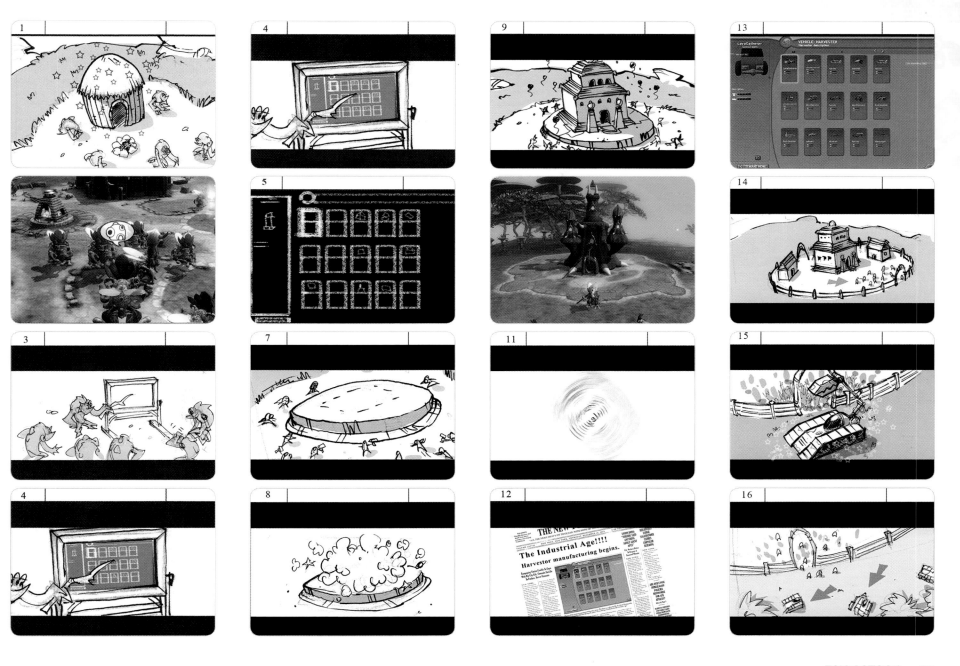

We begin with the player completing the necessary tasks to 'win' tribe game.

The player is asked if they would like to advance, and they select 'yes'

In this example, the Cheiftain begins to talk about WAR. He asks for ideas or suggestions as to how the city could become WARLIKE.

A creeature raises its most readibly available appendage and the Chieftain points to him.

Player enters city hall editor, creates a city hall and clicks 'done'

Return to game and enter LETTERBOX mode. Tribe creatures stand around hut and celebrate the upgrading. Chieftain is near the hut.

'High Supreme Dudeness, like we could totally build, like... tanks!'

The creatures begin to laugh and celebrate! 'Tanks! Dude, that is so AWESOME!' "Yeah, let's build us some killer tanks, bro!"

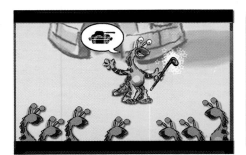

Pull in for close shot of Cheiftain surrounded by his tribal bretheren.

Cut back to shot of Cheiftain. "Tanks... a splendid idea!" Anyone else?

"Your Dudeness... like, wouldn't it be awesome if we mashed together like a jet plane or somethin'... you know, like, to bomb stuff with?"

This goes over even bigger than the tanks. "Dudester, that totally rocks the entire warehouse! Like, wow...jet planes and stuff! Totally gotta do it"

Confused murmuring begins to roll through the crowd.

Cut back to shot of Cheiftain. Confusion reigns.

Cut back to the Cheiftain. "Splendid! Splendid! THat's the spirit! Ww will be killing in no time flat! Who else?"

Another hand is raised...

The cheiftain shakes its head and speaks. "Anyway... WAR...PLANES...TANKS!!!"

The crowd begins to pick up the chant.

Cut back to crowd shot. "Pancakes!"

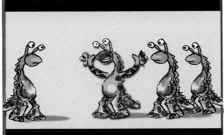

There is dead silence, except for the sound of crickets and a cough from someone 30 ft away. The response giver continues to wave its arms.

4 civilization
stage

We wanted to make a simple strategy game, which can sometimes sound like an oxymoron—simple enough that it wasn't going to put off casual players but complex enough that actual gamers would still find it interesting.

—Alex Hutchinson, Lead Designer: Gameplay

Civ Design

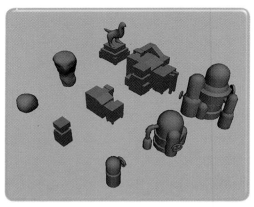

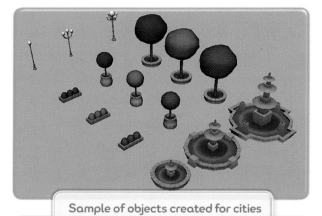

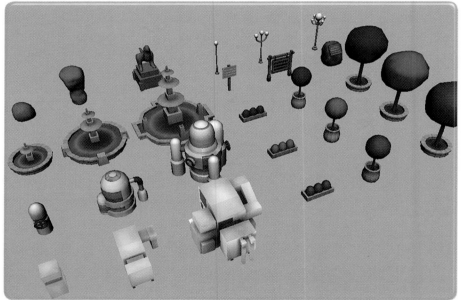

Sample of objects created for cities

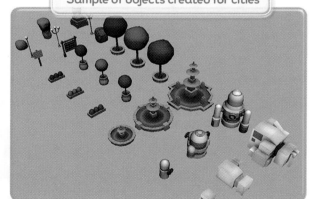

CI_objects_floraContainers_large1.mb
CI_objects_floraContainers_large2.mb
CI_objects_floraContainers_large3.mb
CI_objects_floraContainers_medium1.mb
CI_objects_floraContainers_medium2.mb
CI_objects_floraContainers_medium3.mb
CI_objects_floraContainers_small1.mb
CI_objects_floraContainers_small2.mb
CI_objects_floraContainers_small3.mb
CI_objects_fountain1.mb
CI_objects_fountain2.mb
CI_objects_fountain3.mb
CI_objects_lamp1.mb
CI_objects_lamp2.mb
CI_objects_lamp3.mb
CI_objects_rockLarge.mb
CI_objects_rockMedium.mb
CI_objects_rockSmall.mb
CI_objects_roundGreeble_large.mb
CI_objects_roundGreeble_medium.mb
CI_objects_roundGreeble_small.mb
CI_objects_sign1.mb
CI_objects_sign2.mb
CI_objects_sign3.mb
CI_objects_squareGreeble_large.mb
CI_objects_squareGreeble_medium.mb
CI_objects_squareGreeble_small.mb

This is the level that feels most like a "game" game.
—Soren Johnson, Lead Engineer: Gameplay

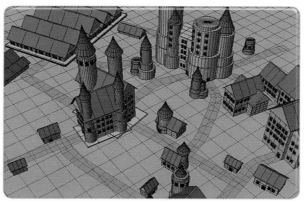

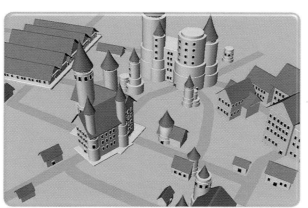

The Civ game presented unique design challenges for the *Spore* team. Based on the fundamentals of the real-time strategy (RTS) genre, it was in many ways more of a challenging game to play than any of the previous phases. At the same time, like all of *Spore*, it was also loaded with opportunities to be creative as it had the most creators of any stage.

For a while there was a sixth stage, the fabled City Stage which was pure city management. Cutting it, as we did, pretty early in development, put a heavy burden on the Civ Stage. Soon after we did it, we realized that the jump from Tribe felt really abrupt. Players move from controlling creatures full time to not controlling creatures at all, with no bridge. In the end, elements of the City Stage crept back into the Civ Stage, in particular the city-building aspect of it, but still the jump from Tribe to Civ is the most abrupt transition in the game.

—ALEX HUTCHINSON, LEAD DESIGNER: GAMEPLAY

Here are early storyboards illustrating the cinematic that would be used to transition the player from the Tribal Stage to the Civ Stage. Considerable care was taken to make this transition as smooth as possible, since it was considered more abrupt than it had been when the City Stage had been part of the game.

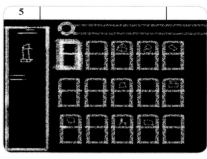

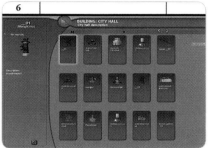

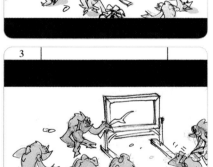

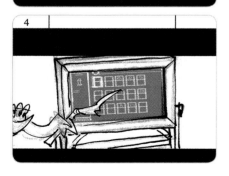

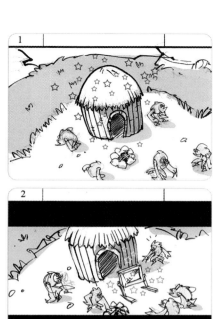

We got rid of City game, and said, okay, we're going right from Tribe to Civ. That's been a bit of a hurdle for us, making the transition really smooth. That was the most jarring moment for players, especially at first when the Tribe had very different controls from Civ. They were so different that when they went from Tribe to controlling land vehicles with a different control scheme and a different camera, it was a little overwhelming. So what we did was bridge ... this large gap in time, which we filled with a transition moment that's actually quite funny. We've been making these transition moments just to ease the player into new stages, and that's been quite a challenge for us. But where we are now is getting people to understand why they have gone from this tribe to where the technology came from, and making it clear you're controlling vehicles now on this level.
—Kip Katsarelis, Producer: Gameplay

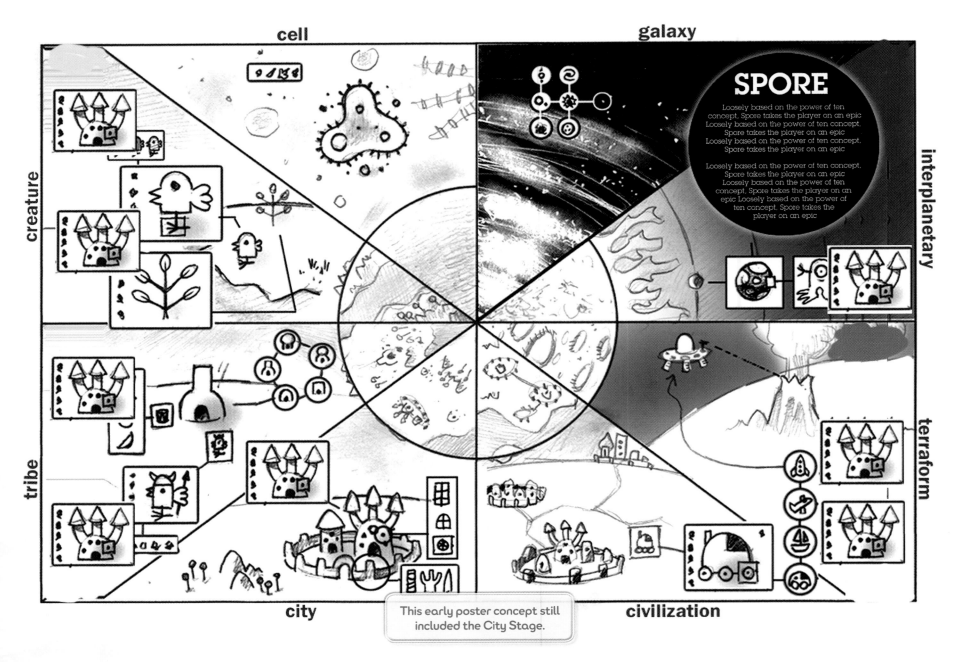

cell

galaxy

SPORE

Loosely based on the power of ten concept, Spore takes the player on an epic Loosely based on the power of ten concept, Spore takes the player on an epic Loosely based on the power of ten concept, Spore takes the player on an epic

Loosely based on the power of ten concept, Spore takes the player on an epic Loosely based on the power of ten concept, Spore takes the player on an epic Loosely based on the power of ten concept, Spore takes the player on an epic

creature

interplanetary

tribe

terraform

city

This early poster concept still included the City Stage.

civilization

We started out imagining Civ to be a cut-down version of *Sid Meier's Civilization*, but it ended up being nothing like that game. We ended up looking at it as more of a game of *Risk*, and bringing out things on the minimap to make it clear that you were owning segments of land and territory really made it pop more. We wanted it to be simple and accessible and as much about looking at your planet, which by this stage is like a big Christmas tree ornament, as it was about hard-core strategy. Toying with your vehicles was as important as using them to win.

—ALEX HUTCHINSON, LEAD DESIGNER: GAMEPLAY

From the get-go, we wanted there to be three strategies in Civ and we wanted them to be different storytelling devices. The idea was you could win religiously, economically, and militarily, and that each one should feel different. Like in all parts of *Spore* we didn't want it to be all aggression all the time. We wanted people to win through positive means as well, which is a challenge in a strategy game because at the end of the day almost all strategy games are about domination and ownership, and these almost always degenerate into combat. So the first prototype for religious, which we decided should have a musical theme, was basically tanks shooting music at buildings and blowing them up, which obviously didn't fit the bill. We ended up with a mechanic whereby the religious vehicles don't destroy cities and instead convert them, but I still wish it felt "friendlier" than it does.

—ALEX HUTCHINSON, LEAD DESIGNER: GAMEPLAY

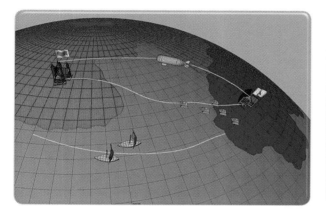

What's really fun is seeing the stuff you created in action, but the Civ game is a land-grab game, with a diplomacy aspect to it. How are you going to interact with your neighbors, for instance? Do you want to be friends with them? Do you want to be not friends with them? We're also trying to make sure the Civ game mirrors the decisions you make at other levels.

—SOREN JOHNSON, LEAD ENGINEER: GAMEPLAY

A religious attack is less destructive to property, but it still results in an all-out battle.

In terms of an arc from Cell to Space, the games essentially get more and more complex and challenging as you move forward. Cell is a very, very simple game, Creature is a little more complex, Tribe has light strategy, but Civ and Space both start to get really quite complicated and "gamey." It's an interesting thing to watch in focus tests, because often we'd see casual users get less interested as the game progressed and gamers become more interested. Hopefully the balancing act pays off and both groups can find enough to love.

—Alex Hutchinson, Lead Designer: Gameplay

Making stuff is fun! The only thing more fun than making stuff is making stuff, then destroying it. *Spore* lets you make the kind of amazing creations you've seen in movies and games. It lets anyone be an artist. It's a creativity amplifier.

—Ocean Quigley, Art Director

In the Civ Stage, once the other nations appear on the map, things get rolling pretty quickly. It's very much a fast-paced RTS, where you're constantly building units, defending your cities, and engaging the NPCs that co-inhabit your planet. We've tried to preserve the terrarium experience you get from some of the earlier levels with subtle details, like customized vignettes and civic object to decorate your cities.

—Kip Katsarelis, Producer: Gameplay

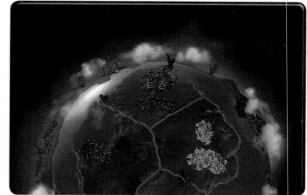

Another hurdle we had in Civ was with the camera. In most of the other levels you're in a very close camera, so you're seeing everything in close, whereas in Civ game you're in close at times, you're at a medium distance, you're at a far distance. Trying to make the game readable, playable, and pretty at all those levels has been difficult. We want to make sure in the near zoom that all the animations are good, interactions are good and appealing, and all the citizens, if you get close to a city, they are all doing their individual animations with one another. You can see that when you're up close; however, when you pull back you kind of lose that detail. So we go to a more iconic representation of all that stuff you saw. In the near zoom for combat, for example, you see detailed explosions—you'll see citizens flying from the vehicles and it feels like you're in this war zone. Then you pull back to the far zoom and see tiny explosions and little iconic representations of all this fiasco that's going on.

Your citizens protest all the time, so when you get in close you will see them stomping around, yelling at your city hall and asking for things. When you pull back, you still get the chants, but you get these little flashing sign boards over our city, which are just iconic versions of those citizens. Whenever we're thinking about game design in Civ, we're always thinking about what that near zoom experience is going to be and what that far zoom experience is going to be, and it's all got to be tight and cohesive, and playable at both those zooms. One of the things we found was, depending on the player (and it doesn't matter if they are a casual gamer or a hard-core gamer), different people play at different zoom levels. So once in a while you will see someone play the entire game at the closest zoom, and they are able to play that game at that zoom. They have UI and minimap help to help them navigate the globe. Then you see other players who play the whole game at the far zoom, so you never know. To each his own, I guess.

—Kip Katsarelis, Producer: Gameplay

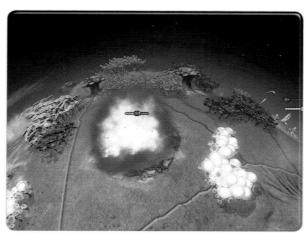

The Tactical Nuke military super weapon

The Mighty Bomb
military super weapon

The Invulnerability military super weapon

The Healing Aura religious super weapon

The Diplomatic Dervish
economic super weapon

The Bribes & Confusion
economic super weapon

The Black Cloud economic super weapon

What you do in each of the levels will have ramifications to what happens in the Civ game. The biggest effects come from Tribe. The way you play Tribe determines which of the three paths you start out with—military, religious, or economic. If you're a really aggressive tribe, you'll start out as a military civilization. But we also have this concept of super weapons, which are big global powers that you can build up and use. They can be anything from a napalm strike if you're militaristic, or a global ad blitz if you're trying to win them over to your side. We have things like healing powers or powers that make your units invulnerable. You might use bribery to make the other units fight each other, and these are all things that are based upon what we call "consequences," but basically they are based on what you have achieved in the earlier levels. So, as an example, if you're an omnivore cell, you might get the invulnerability super power when you get to Civ.

—Soren Johnson, Lead Engineer: Gameplay

There was always lots to do in Civ game—you could edit buildings, edit creatures, make nine different types of vehicles—all of which were fine and fun to do. But why stop there? We found that users were spending much of their time waiting for their units to carry out orders, without much else to do in between. And we thought, wouldn't it be fun if you could be part of the conflict and help out in some of these battles directly? This is where super weapons came in. You could go and build your vehicles, then send your toys into battle and assist them with a Healing Aura or Invulnerability or Gadget Bomb a group of enemy tanks and watch them blow into bits. Everyone likes explosions, don't they?

—Kip Katsarelis,
Producer: Gameplay

The Ad Blitz economic super weapon

Originally the super weapons began because a lot of RTS games share this problem where the last 15 minutes is not very fun because you're just mopping up and things just get more and more overwhelming. So we wanted something like the super weapons to solve that problem. And then we branched out from there and thought it would be nice to have these minor super weapons that you could use more piecemeal. And at the end of the day, we're not really interested in the AI beating the player. So we didn't have to worry about how the AI would use these super weapons. I mean it would probably be pretty frustrating if the player's moving along well and suddenly all of their units are attacking each other, or something like that.

—Soren Johnson, Lead Engineer: Gameplay

Epics

One of the things that emerged in *Spore*'s Creature game was the idea of "epic" creatures. "What if we scaled up creatures and made them really large?" We were going after this *Jurassic Park* kind of moment. So an engineer scaled up some creatures, and they were very funny, like these giant Macy's Day Parade balloons. They didn't animate well and looked a little broken, but they were fun.... Once the animators got a hold of them and specialized their animations, we were in business.

Well, once they went in, of course everyone was like "Wow! This is really cool! Can we put them in Tribe?" We all thought it would be cool for the tribes to attack epics and vice versa. Of course we couldn't stop there. In Civ game they wanted to introduce epics, which sparks memories of Godzilla attacking Tokyo. Epics are an interesting piece of game play, kind of like a roaming disaster, pinballing around the map. You never know where it's going to stop and turn its destruction on next.

Sometimes an epic will attack a vehicle. It appears to get mad at that vehicle, and then some random vehicle just runs over to it and kills it, which isn't necessarily how we wanted it to work. It's quite funny when you see this massive epic getting run over by a tiny vehicle. Even the Space game has them now. They can attack cities and spaceships, and you can grab them and put them down on planets to wreak havoc. Epics have been a ton of fun.

—Kip Katsarelis, Producer: Gameplay

Civ Concept Sketches

Themes and Feeds

We offer filters for the players. When they are playing the game, they can elect to leave it all open, or they can elect to ban content they don't like. They can subscribe to certain feeds that other players have made. They can say, for example, "I want to play the game in a hard-core science fiction way." They can find feeds other players have made, like scary-looking space vehicles and aliens, and subscribe to it. We figure there is going to be a vast aesthetic range, not just good and practical, but things that are good and "Whoa!"

There's someone who put together a feed of buildings for the Civ game that are all baked goods, with cupcake houses and a birthday cake for a city hall. You can have cities that look like collections of baked goods by subscribing to the right feed.

—Ocean Quigley, Art Director

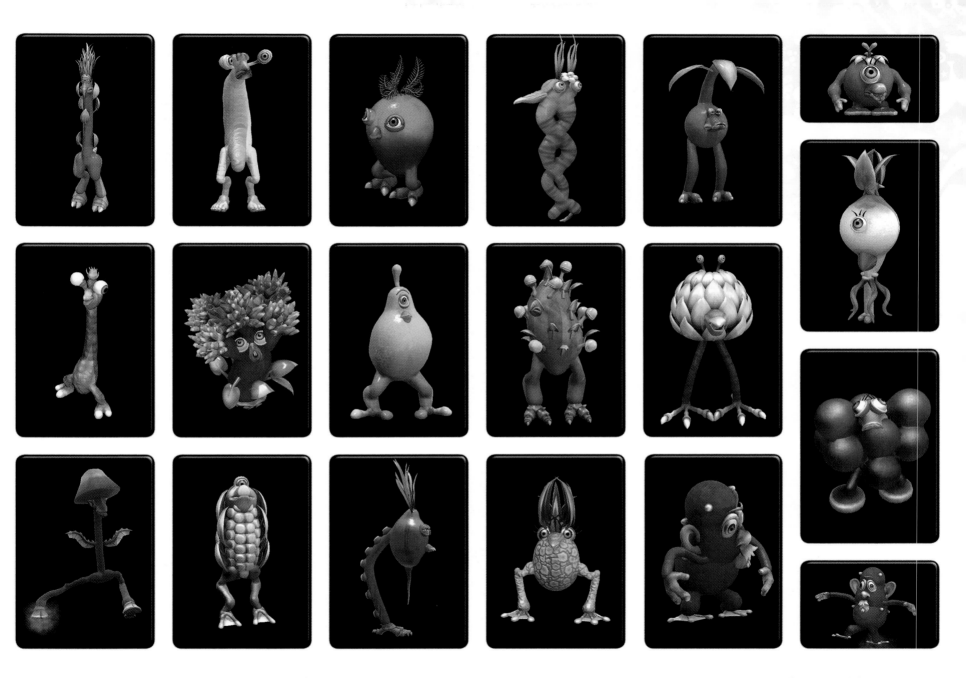

Civ Creators

The Civ Stage features creators for land, air, and sea vehicles, and buildings; it's a builder/designer's paradise.

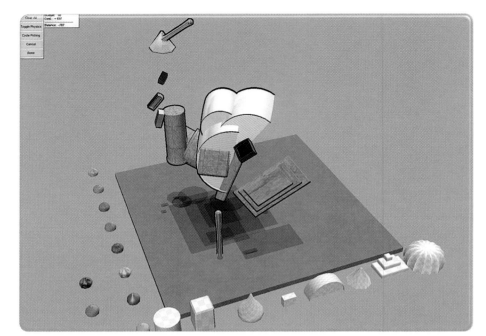

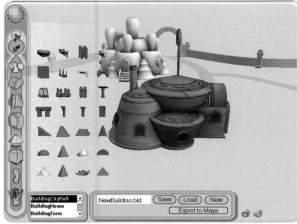

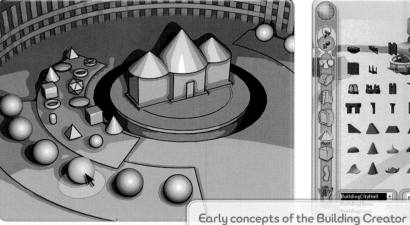

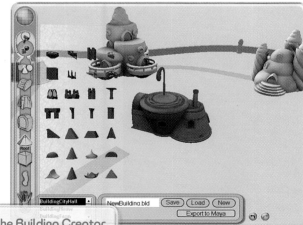

Early concepts of the Building Creator

Testing different paint jobs for buildings

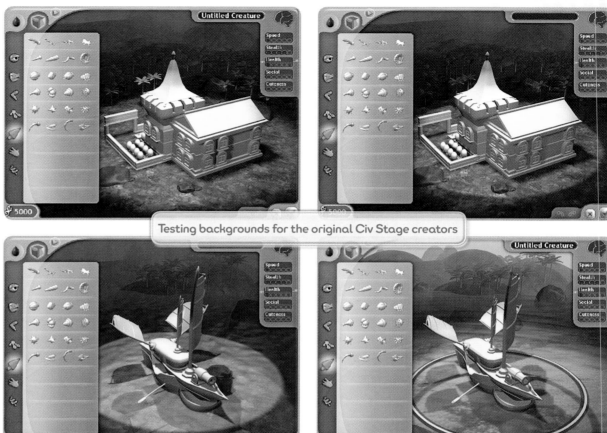

Testing backgrounds for the original Civ Stage creators

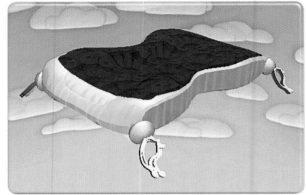

Interestingly, even though players can create all kinds of vehicles in the Civ Stage, it's not as personal as creating a creature. We struggled a lot with trying to add effects and animation to make vehicles feel as fun and toy-like and alive as the creatures, but it was a very difficult problem. There's just something about the moment your creation turns and looks at you that connects you to it, like a puppy, and with a vehicle we just couldn't do it. Maybe we could have stuck eyeballs on the bumpers or something. We had a similar problem with the buildings, which just felt inert at first—you built them and then they just sat there. We had grand ideas for creatures going in and out of doors, or sitting on balconies, but again with the freedom that the Building Creator provides and the vast variety of creatures you can make, it just wasn't feasible. Maybe in *Spore 2*!

—Alex Hutchinson, Lead Designer: Gameplay

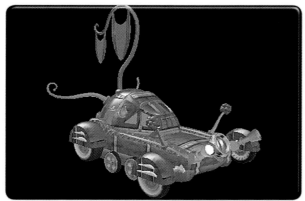

Vehicles might not be as "personal" as creatures, but the team managed to make them interesting.

Civ Models

How you play the Civ game can also influence how you start in the Space game. They have nine archetypes that you can start the Space game with, and that affects the tools you start off with and a bunch of other things. Because players have four levels behind them, it's hard for the designers on Space to figure out all the mappings, but each level does factor into that.

—Soren Johnson, Lead Engineer: Gameplay

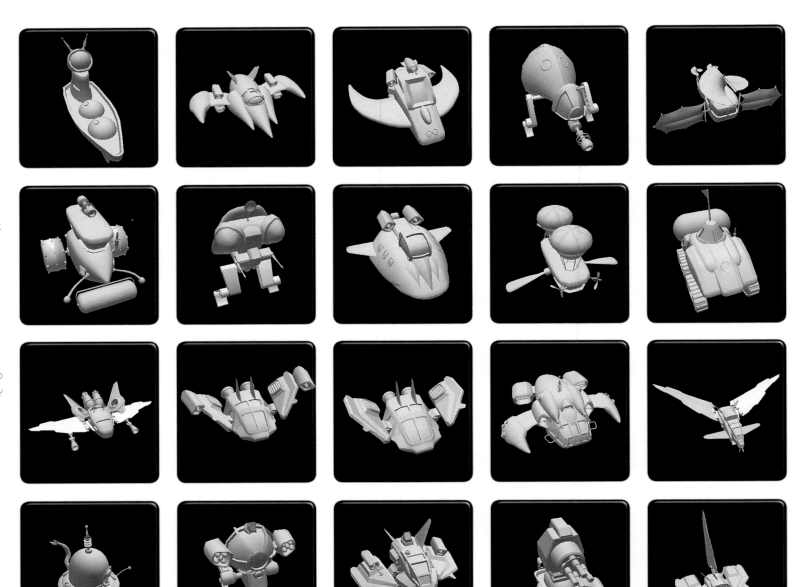

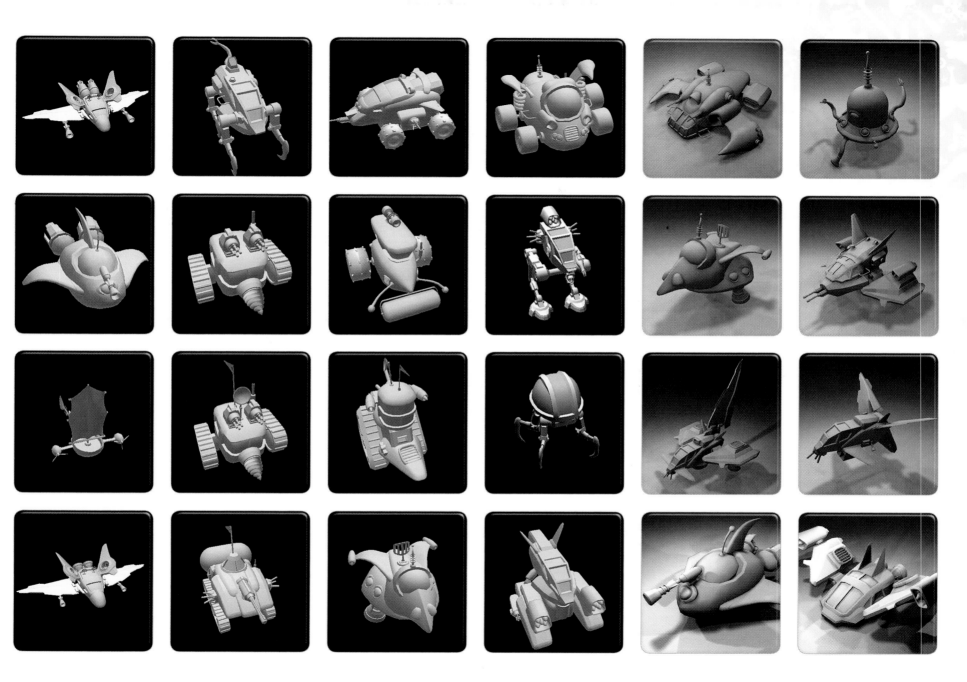

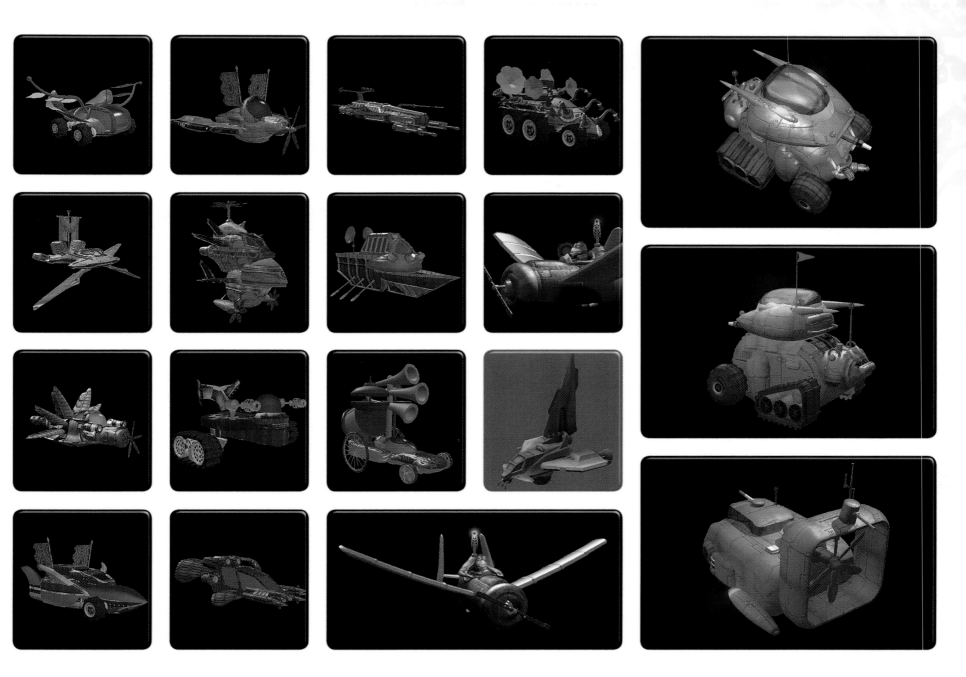

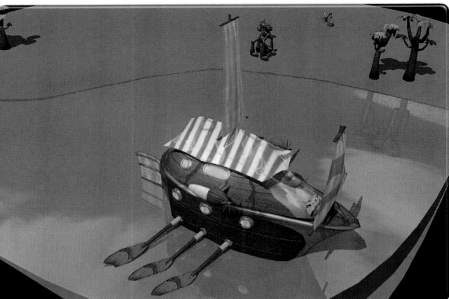

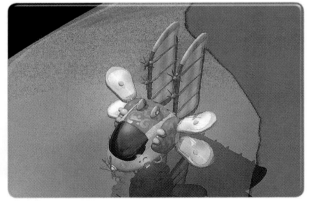

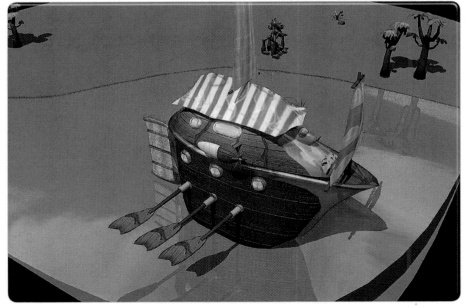

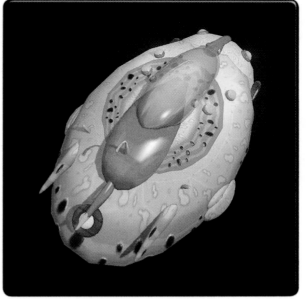

With buildings and vehicles, the most amazing moment came when we were able to create something in the editors, texture it, then take it into another 3-D program, render it with lighting and effects and stuff.... After spending years creating assets the hard way, seeing how easy it was to create buildings or a bunch of vehicles for an army, and then dumping them into a scene—I was just blown away by that.

—MIKE KHOURY, LEAD ARTIST

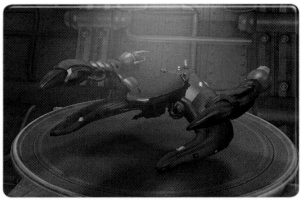
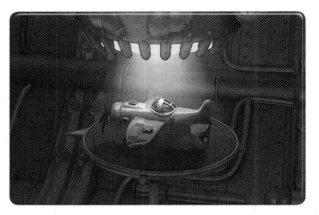

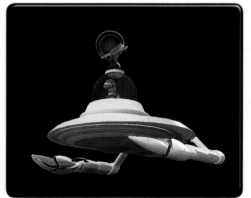
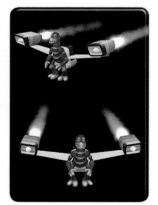

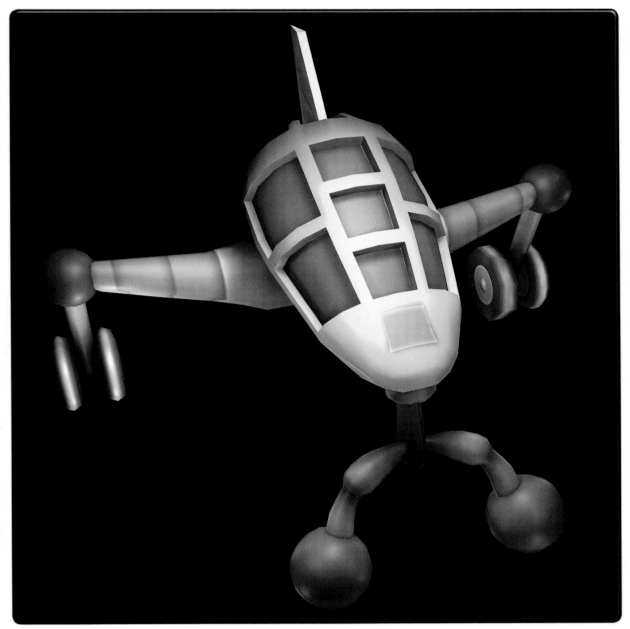

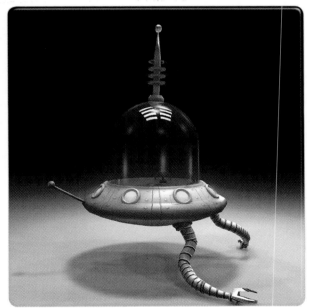

Early on we did lots of brain storming with Will. His whole drive on the rig blocks ... was to use unrecognizable platonic shapes. He was more interested in giving the player cones and spheres and cubes, and letting the player build a castle out of that, than us making it too easy for the player or trying to guide them too much.... But what we noticed from looking at the database of stuff people created, was, wow, a lot of this stuff just looks like crap. Someone would stack three cubes and throw a triangle on the end and paint it.... [We thought,] is this what we're going to get? ... So we started designing things that looked like building blocks and had a function built into them.... We built them with a specific deforms in mind, a uniform, consistent, and predictable approach for the player, but our mantra has always been, "variety, variety, variety."

—MIKE KHOURY, LEAD ARTIST

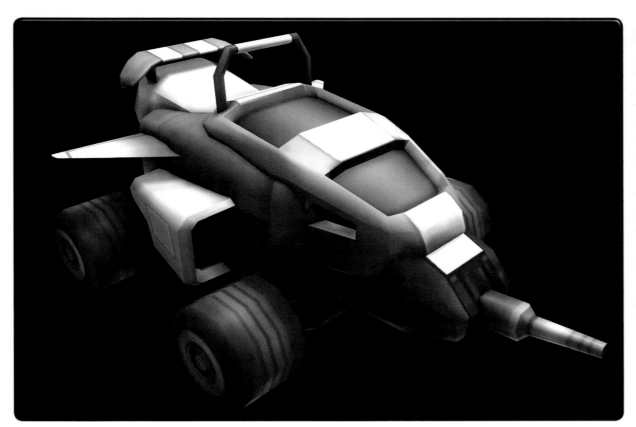

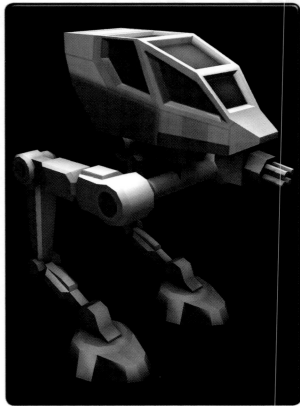

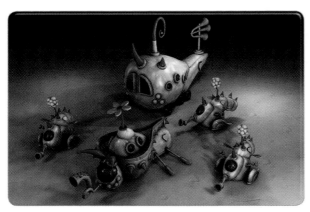

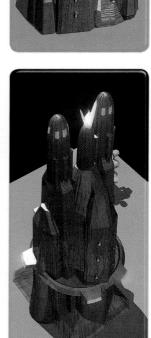

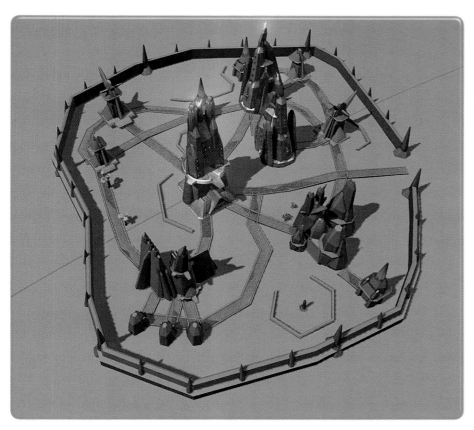

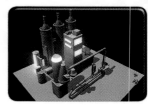

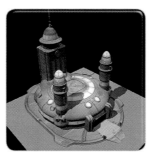

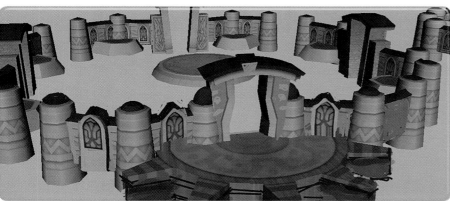

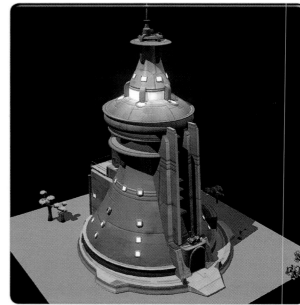

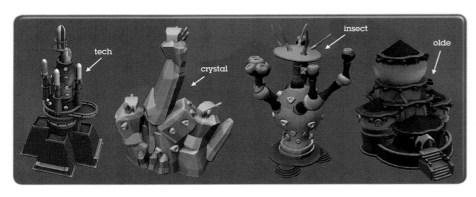

tech

crystal

insect

olde

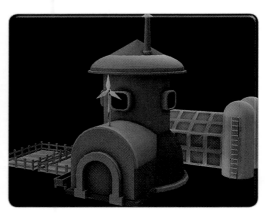

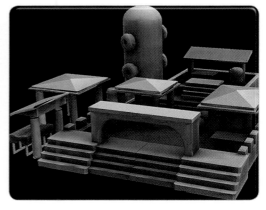

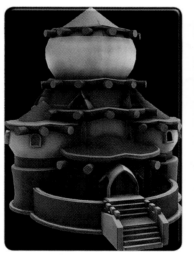

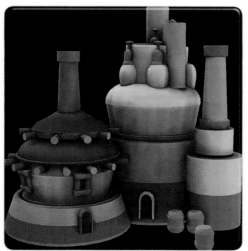

A basic description of rig blocks would be little deformable blocks—almost like little transformer blocks—that you can put together in any way you want to make different shapes.

—MIKE KHOURY, LEAD ARTIST

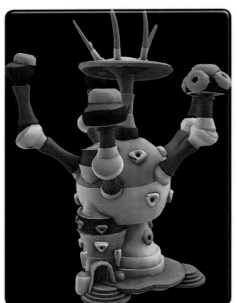

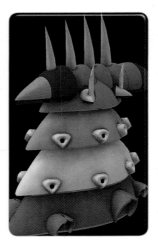

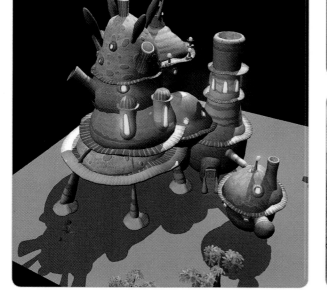

Getting Really Creative

When they tackled the creators in the Civ Stage, the *Spore* team's creative talent and wackiness found the perfect vehicle—so to speak—of expression. Here are some examples of how they continually stretched the boundaries of expectation in each of the Civ creators.

do you want to evolve?

yes or no

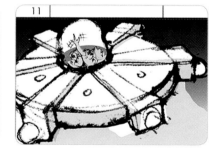

viewing shields

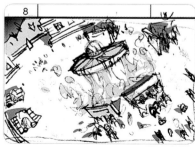

Something that became apparent to me during development was that the journey to Space from Cell had to be relatively short. Even though the narrative from Cell to Space was epic, the game time had to be short, and the reason for that is that if your game is all about content, by implication it's all about replayablity. If you're only going to go through it once, we've wasted our time building all these creators, because you just won't see a lot of content.

In Space the content is less intimate. You're not standing up next to a creature that's looking at you from three feet away. As you move through *Spore* it's essentially a process of pulling back, in physical terms, in terms of control and in terms of your relationship to your avatar. First, you're controlling a single creature, then a group of guys, and eventually you're essentially God in a spaceship. And I think the key is that all of these are happening in sync and the camera is pulling back farther and farther, and when it all works together, it has to be short to have that impact of epic scope and scale. I personally really wanted a player to be able to wake up on a Sunday morning and play all the way from Cell to Space that day, and then want to do it again tomorrow with different stuff.

It was funny that when we announced that *Spore* was actually pretty short from Cell to Space, some game websites sort of lost their collective minds because they thought we were saying that *Spore* was five hours long. Of course it's not, but it's interesting that a game is often judged by its play time. For some, "epic" means long, but for us "epic" means vast. Our game is all about breadth, not depth—infinite content, huge scope, but simple gameplay. That was our mantra for all levels, except Space a little bit.

—Alex Hutchinson, Lead Designer: Gameplay

5 space
stage

The Space Stage is a giant sand box, interwoven with a light RPG, and it's HUGE. You start off on your home planet that you've been playing on possibly since Cell game. You're given a Space Ship that you create and control. The ship is your avatar and will carry you across the stars, taking you on countless adventures. It's up to you to take part in the story line, choose to make your mark in the galaxy by expanding your Empire, colonize new worlds, and interact with strange sentient life forms. Along the way you'll earn badges that will unlock new and interesting tools, while tracking your progress. Or you might want to simply explore the depths of space at your own pace, using some of the more creative tools. For instance, with the aesthetic tool sets, you can become a planet Picasso. Essentially painting different planets, sculpting their terrain, changing the color of the oceans and atmosphere, all from the safety of your space ship. There's an endless amount of creativity to be had, that's really a lot of fun.

—Kip Katsarelis, Producer: Gameplay

The Final Frontier

Space is truly the final frontier in *Spore*, providing a vast sandbox for play and exploration. We really didn't want each evolutionary stage to last forever. We wanted to get the player to space, as it's an important part of our game. There's plenty of game before that, but we really wanted players to feel the full arch of their evolution.

—MATT POWERS, PRODUCER: GAMEPLAY

We're trying to perform a scale inversion of cosmic proportions. Turn everything inside out: Transform the huge, frightening, and awesome universe into something smooth, small, and delicate. A fragile seedling a child will hold and be charmed by. A smooth round seed, a game, which contains the vastness of the universe, the massive stampede of life, and the incomprehensible magnitude of evolution.

—CHAIM GINGOLD, DESIGNER: CREATORS

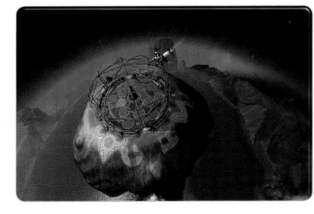

"You can become a planet Picasso."

—KIP KATSARELIS, PRODUCER: GAMEPLAY

Instead of becoming an abstract and intellectual game for astrobiologists and rocket scientists, *Spore* mutated into something more down-to-earth. You could explain the concept to almost anybody: Make your own creature, take over the planet, and explore space, where you'll meet space aliens made by other players. Who wouldn't want to do that? In retrospect, the original inchoate vastness of *Spore* needed to be folded into a user-friendly conformation, one that would invite ordinary people to pick it up and play.

—CHAIM GINGOLD, DESIGNER: CREATORS

We're finding that players are not taking the constraints of the game too seriously. For example, if you go to the UFO Creator, you can make spaceships like you've seen in movies and TV shows and real life. But other people have made Whistler's Mother, literally, as a UFO. You just recognize it right off the bat.

Somebody made a fruit bowl as a UFO. Another made a four-poster bed. I don't know what you do with people like that! They're making something wonderful. They're getting aesthetic control and doing what they want to do with it, but how am I supposed to make a four-poster bed look like a scary space vehicle?

—Ocean Quigley, Art Director

One really fun exchange we had with the community was when we decided to make a Flash movie that tried to represent the concept of *Spore*. We wanted it to be fun and ended up producing an iconic look—it's black and white—in a piece that expresses the stages of the game on the journey from cell to space. We released this movie on our website, and very shortly after that, we found that people in the community started using that art as personal icons. One fan started creating new icons, based on the look of the movie, to depict what he imagined the game could possibly feature. Mitosis. Love triangles. Teen pregnancy. Warfare. Mutations. Just a crazy amount of things, all represented in this iconic style that was riffing off the movie that we had made. I found these on *GamingSteve*, and people were commenting back on these icons further developing the ideas that they expressed. It was an interesting look inside the heads of our potential players, what they had heard about the game, where they were imagining it going. I started tracking how many of these things we were covering in the game, how many things we were missing, and it was fun to see that if we just did a little bit we might be able to capture that fantasy of life. It was an interesting pre-design process.

—Lucy Bradshaw, Executive Producer

Maxis Goes to the Stars

Then, there is the problem of aliens. Popular alien narratives focus on the friction of human/alien contact.... But the really interesting design question about first contact that *Spore* poses is not the traditional one. Earthlings always identify with the home team, whether that's humans fighting off space invaders or a family going about its life in a *Sims* subdivision.... *Spore's* dilemma was simple: People readily identify with people, but could we get them to do the same for aliens?

Of course, these aren't any old aliens we ask players to invest in—they're your creation, your aliens. Once you start customizing, and design your creature, emotional investment is generated. It's magic. Even the ugly ones are loved by their parents. Many games thrive on the interest generated by players' creative investment. Console role-playing games, for example, get this effect when players invest time in equipping and naming characters. I've always felt more attached to my characters as I fuss over their outfits and equipment. Creative interaction seems to always generate emotional involvement and attachment.

—Chaim Gingold, Designer: Creators

Battle in this 3D world was posing a unique challenge, and I literally have a four square ball in my room, [and we would use it], imagining the little UFO moving over it and using it to visualize the way it would work.

—Jenna Chalmers, Designer: Gameplay

-12-

-13-

-14-

-15-

-16-

-17-

-18-

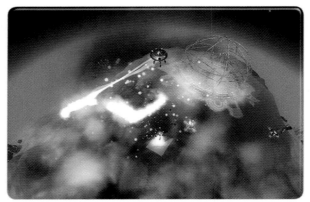

We started off in the Space game asking ourselves, "If you could be the space guy what would you want to do?" And we broke down all these high-level concepts of what someone would want to do in space. Would they want to conquer? Would they want to explore? For sure they would want to discover new species or make friends. All these high-level ideas were well documented in sci-fi. But there's more. Would I want to make crop circles? Would I want to terrorize people? Would I want to abduct things? Kind of this very high-level classic UFO behavior, classic alien behavior. And then we tried to piece those together into a gameplay that had structure and checks and balances, and ultimately the storyline becomes that you're this little creature and you've evolved on your own little planet, and you've been developing your own little transportation, and developing your species and your buildings, and at the last stage you become a unifying planet—you have resolved all your global conflicts and you blast off into space, and now you've got this whole vast universe to explore. At that point the game's objectives become really defined by the player, like all Maxis games. So do you want to be a large empire? Do you define success by a lot of qualities, or do you define success by the amount of space you've explored—that you've traveled through the farthest reaches? ... The Space game, ultimately, your goal is to expand in some way, and how you define that growth and expansion is up to you.

—JENNA CHALMERS, DESIGNER: GAMEPLAY

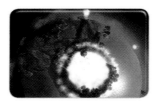

This is going to sound clichéd—but space is vast. Sure, that's obvious, but that vastness posed challenge after challenge that I don't think we, or at least I, thought about until we really got in there. When you have that many planets and that many stars to work with, very simple things become very complicated. For instance, if you want something to be rare—a creature, an artifact, a rare planet that has special properties or has special value to the player—it's very challenging to make something rare. Either it's a needle in a haystack they will never find, or it's not really that rare. And in theory you can play the numbers [but] there was very little we could do to guarantee that the player would hit the sweet spot of the tuning.... And ultimately a lot of gameplay comes down to how hard or easy is something to find, whether it's a rare or a valuable planet, or a valuable ally.... It just becomes very challenging to control what happens in that much space.

—JENNA CHALMERS, DESIGNER: GAMEPLAY

"Our ship has spotted a rare, Captain!"

chest armor with built in nueral processor

forearm prosthesis

helmet imagi...

Exoskeleton grasper

exoskeleton foot

An earlier version of the Grox that didn't make the cut.

This version of the Grox, with top hat and cane, was done just for laughs.

We designed the Space game so you can play it according any number of play styles; as a warmonger, for instance, or a colonizer or explorer. Your goal was to make it to the center of the galaxy and achieve Master Badge level 10. There was an adversary you would meet along the way and we wanted to keep it all hush-hush at first. The adversary was the "Grox," and they were hell-bent on destroying everyone in the galaxy. They lived on barren planets with no atmosphere, and that's how they like it. So they will go convert other planets to T-Zeros and destroy anyone in their path. It's usually best advised to stay out of their radar early on.

Spore is all about creativity and sharing ones creations. In Space we take the content from all the levels, creatures, vehicles, buildings, spaceships, and package it all on planets that you get to visit in a spaceship you created. When I said Space was large, I wasn't kidding. You start out on your solar system, which usually contains roughly three planets. There might be 70,000 stars in your galaxy, all of which might contain a number of planets to go visit. Each one of those planets is guaranteed to contain new and unique content. You could go visit civ planets, other space-faring planets, tribe planets etc., and you can interact with those planets. This is where you begin to see the terrarium game unfold, watching the Tribe Stage play out in front of you. You can get out of you spaceship, where anything can happen. They may look up at you in fear, they may worship you, maybe you'll cook them with you laser, or abduct them for later use. And let's not forget our tools. We can't have a space game without weapons, so you can blow up all the cool stuff you discover. There are missiles, pulse weapons, lasers, planet busters, and more. You can paint the ground with your lasers and lay waste to the entire planet in a matter of minute. It never gets old.

—Kip Katsarelis, Producer: Gameplay

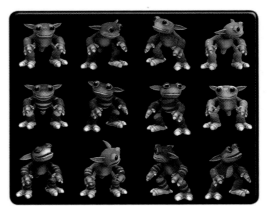

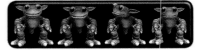

Scale and Views

Transitioning from long views to close views was a challenge. I think there are still definite transition points that don't cross fade well.... So what we try to do is make the steps between these transitions from a high-resolution model to a simpler proxy of that model similar enough that you don't really notice the discontinuity. But there are transitions we can't match very well. As you zoom out, the transition from a 3-D model to a little flat picture of that model (a tree for example) is something that you can still see in game. We really can't match that any better with our performance constraints. So what we tried to do is make that transition far enough from the camera and apply some fog and lighting tricks to minimize the impact on the viewer.

—Christian Stratton, Effects and Technical Artist

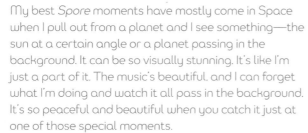

My best *Spore* moments have mostly come in Space when I pull out from a planet and I see something—the sun at a certain angle or a planet passing in the background. It can be so visually stunning. It's like I'm just a part of it. The music's beautiful, and I can forget what I'm doing and watch it all pass in the background. It's so peaceful and beautiful when you catch it just at one of those special moments.

—Jenna Chalmers, Designer: Gameplay

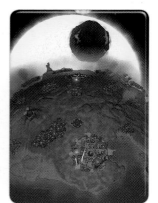

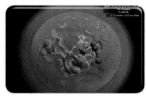

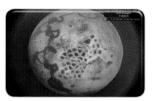

Making Planets and Landscapes

Planet Scripting

We had a couple of different and competing philosophies related to how to create planets. The core philosophy of the game design is to make everything procedural and kind of bubble up from a few little rule sets, and that's beauty of the galaxy—we populate this game with so many little AI things that give you something to look at. Everything is fresh and new and everybody's experience can be different. Then we have some of our more seasoned artists who wanted to have more control—to be sure every planet was beautiful.... But of course we can't really do both at the same time.

Then at one point we had an epiphany. We were breaking down, pulling our hair out, and suddenly this system idea popped into a few of our heads, and we immediately went off to tear apart the planet system and rebuild it from scratch. And this was a system where we create parts of terrains, or features that are partially random, partially not, working within constraints, but then someone goes in and places these on the planet, so the planet becomes an artist's assemblage of semi-random but contained components. Once that clicked, and we started making examples, we knew we had something. This was a way planets could be different from one to the next, but we had enough control over where things went, where an ocean went, or where a mountain range went. Although we didn't know the form of the ocean or mountain range, we could at least guarantee that things would appear at the right percentages, that one thing wouldn't dig in and make something else really horrible, or clash with it...but still allow the randomness to come through. The new planets were so much easier to author and so much more interesting that within 2[EN]3 weeks of having that lightbulb turn on, we had a growing library of these new planets in game. It was a real turning point for us.

—CHRISTIAN STRATTON, EFFECTS AND TECHNICAL ARTIST

Testing scripted planets for percentage of land vs. water

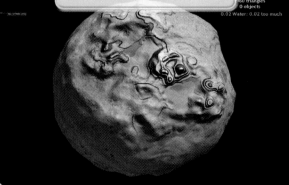

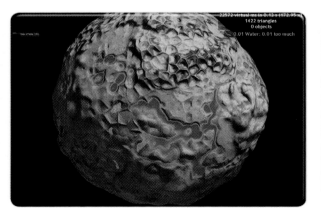

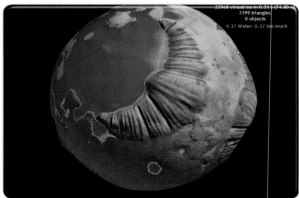

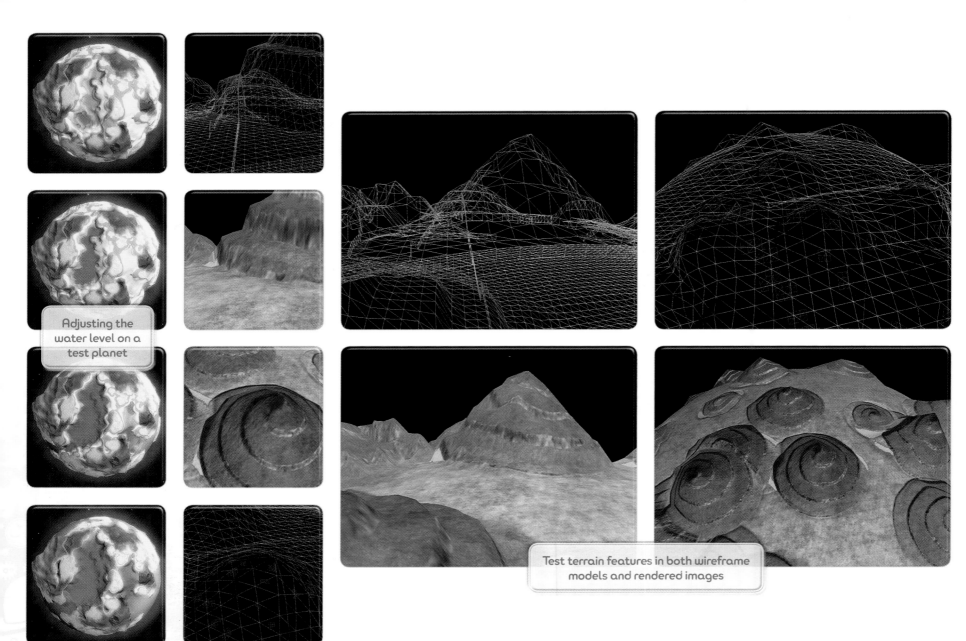

Adjusting the water level on a test planet

Test terrain features in both wireframe models and rendered images

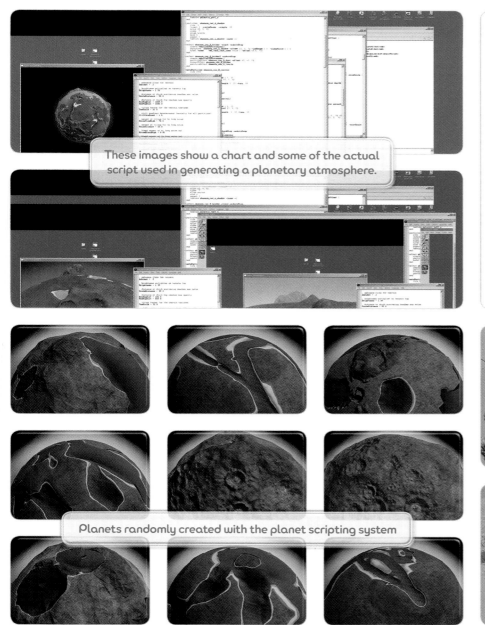

These images show a chart and some of the actual script used in generating a planetary atmosphere.

Planets randomly created with the planet scripting system

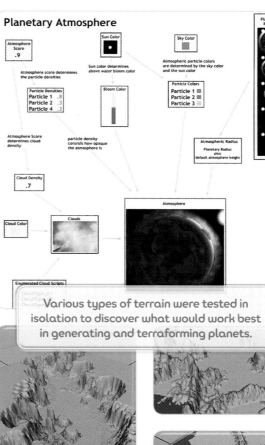

Planetary Atmosphere

Atmosphere Score
.9

Atmosphere score determines the particle densities

Particle Densities
Particle 1 .8
Particle 2 .3
Particle 4 .2

Atmosphere Score determines cloud density

Cloud Density
.7

Cloud Color

Clouds

Sun Color

Sun color determines above water bloom color

Bloom Color

particle density controls how opaque the atmosphere is

Sky Color

Atmospheric particle colors are determined by the sky color and the sun color

Particle Colors
Particle 1
Particle 2
Particle 3

Atmospheric Radius
Planetary Radius plus
default atmosphere height

Planetary Radius

Atmosphere

Enumerated Cloud Scripts
CloudType_01
CloudType
CloudType

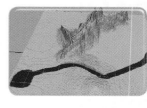

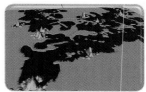

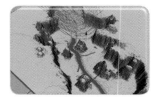

Various types of terrain were tested in isolation to discover what would work best in generating and terraforming planets.

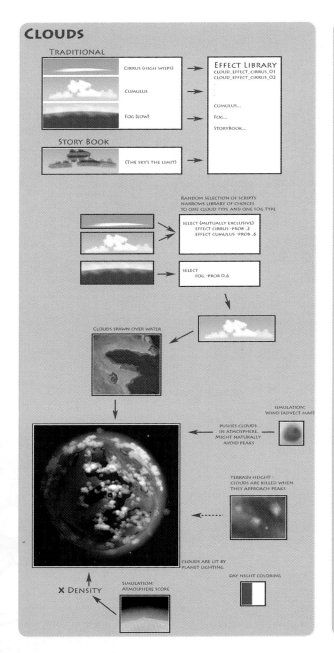

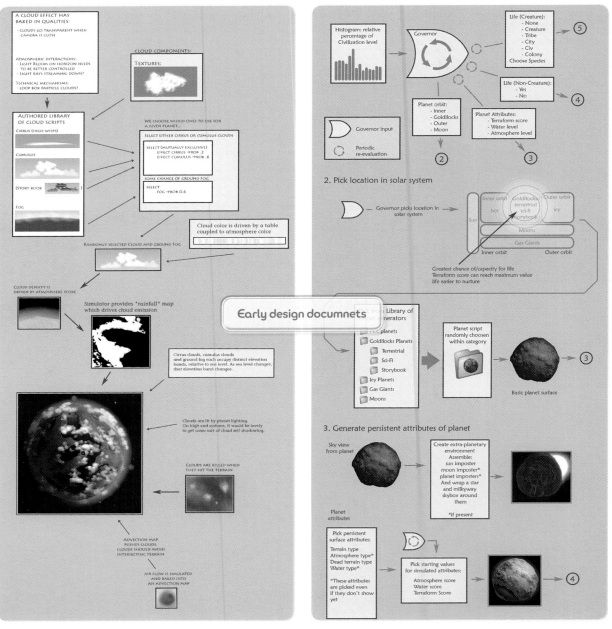

Early design documnets

How tools appear in the Terrain Editor

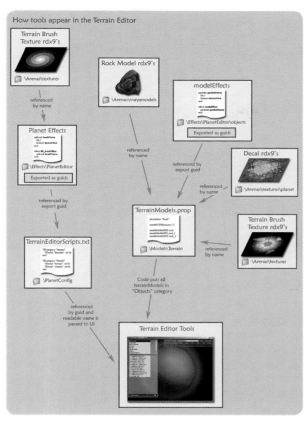

Terrain Brush Texture rdx9's
\Arenas\textures

referenced by name

Planet Effects
\Effects\PlanetEditor
Exported as guids

referenced by export guid

TerrainEditorScripts.txt
\PlanetConfig

referenced by guid and readable name is passed to UI

Rock Model rdx9's
\Arenas\mayamodels

referenced by name

modelEffects
\Effects\PlanetEditor\objects
Exported as guids

referenced by export guid

Decal rdx9's
\Arenas\texture\planet

referenced by name

TerrainModels.prop
description "Rock"
modelLODSources 1 2
modelLODALOD1 rock
modelLODALOD1 rock_1
modelLODALOD1 rock_2
\Models\Terrain

referenced by name

Terrain Brush Texture rdx9's
\Arenas\textures

Code puts all terrainModels in "Objects" category

Terrain Editor Tools

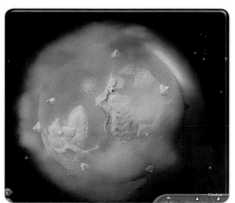

Original. Temp .5, atmosphere .5

After setting atmosphere to 0. Note that we're still seeing fully terraformed color

after setting temperature to 0. Looks good.

setting temperature back to .5. Atmosphere at 0. note green, even though terraform level is still 0. And trees. And water.

Setting temperature and atmosphere to .5 note how it's different from the original temperature and atmosphere .5 (more dead color)

Setting Temp. to 1. Looks good.

Setting atmosphere to 0. Note trees...

Setting atmosphere to 1 and temperature to .5 note that we're still seeing some green.

Rocks, Flowers, Trees, and Other Planetary Phenomena

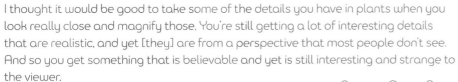

Ocean Quigley's reference photos, used to help conceptualize *Spore*'s flora.

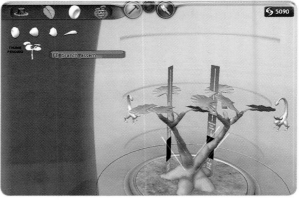

I thought it would be good to take some of the details you have in plants when you look really close and magnify those. You're still getting a lot of interesting details that are realistic, and yet [they] are from a perspective that most people don't see. And so you get something that is believable and yet is still interesting and strange to the viewer.

—Shannon Galvin, Artist

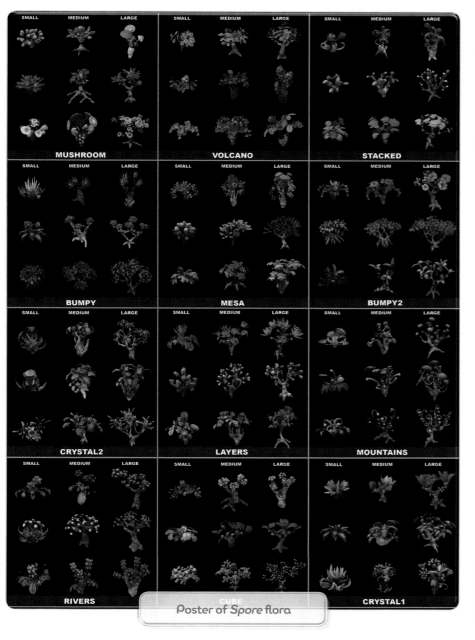

SMALL	MEDIUM	LARGE	SMALL	MEDIUM	LARGE	SMALL	MEDIUM	LARGE
	MUSHROOM			VOLCANO			STACKED	
	BUMPY			MESA			BUMPY2	
	CRYSTAL2			LAYERS			MOUNTAINS	
	RIVERS			CUBE			CRYSTAL1	

Poster of *Spore* flora

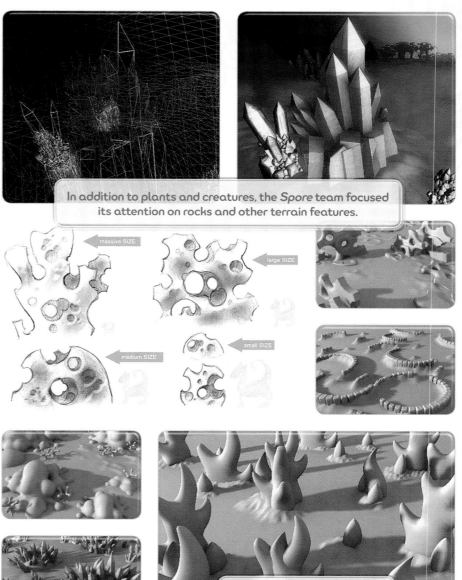

In addition to plants and creatures, the *Spore* team focused its attention on rocks and other terrain features.

massive SIZE

large SIZE

medium SIZE

small SIZE

This terrain concept was inspired by a rooting potato.

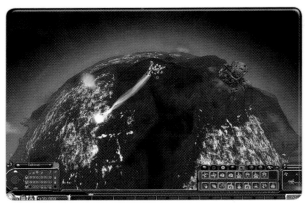 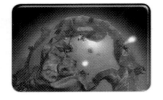 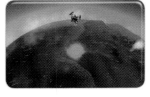  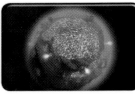

 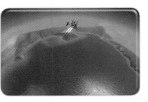  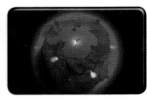

   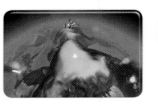 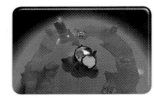

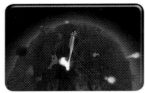   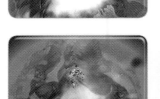 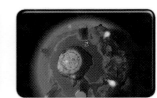 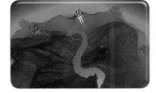 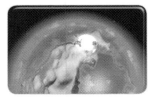 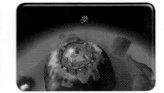

I would say the most creative aspect in the Space game for the player is the planet sculpting—molding planets, and being able to build this whole world. That means a few things. It can mean using these artistic tools that literally mold the planet, color the planet, carve mountains or make swirls—this kind of artist in a box, as we like to call it. It's pure godlike skills. You're molding the planet to be the planet you want it to be. It's very creative, and very satisfying to use your UFO to paint this world.

There's another part that's half creative and half gameplay, which takes it further, which is found in the terraforming tools which are different from the artistic tools. These tools do things like make the planet hotter or colder, or change the atmosphere from having sparse or dense atmosphere. Based on how you use those tools, that dictates how many plants and animals you can put on the planet.

Then you get to the third level of creativity. Now I've got this planet that I've got to the ice temperature or the atmospheric conditions that I want, and now what do I want to populate it with—what kinds of plants or animals? You've explored the galaxy, maybe, and picked up other peoples' creations or edited or created your own. So those two parts, the controlling atmosphere and temperature, and adding plants and animals, all have gameplay repercussions. It's a really special blend of creative things, and that carries over into gameplay features.

—JENNA CHALMERS, DESIGNER: GAMEPLAY

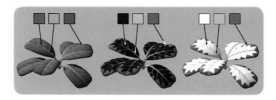

FOREST TYPES

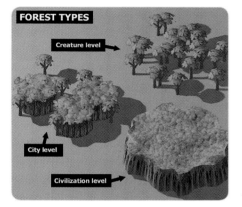

Creature level

City level

Civilization level

In creating the planet system, we had lots of areas of focus: like the terrain texture system—cliffs, valleys, ridges and water; like flora—where and how grass and trees appear, what they look like and what that tells you about a particular planet. These have been really interesting challenges and have had their difficulties along the way as well. The terrain system, it's topology and it's texturing system, is now actually pretty beautiful, but the design really stumbled along for a long period of time as we struggled to keep different cliff textures, beach textures and other surface patterns that appeared depending on the context of the topography. Many of these were things that we had to either abandon or really simplify in the end.... There were a lot of things we had to bang our heads against and chip away at over the course of years, not months like you would expect from other projects.

—Christian Stratton,
Effects and Technical Artist

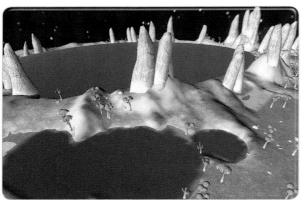

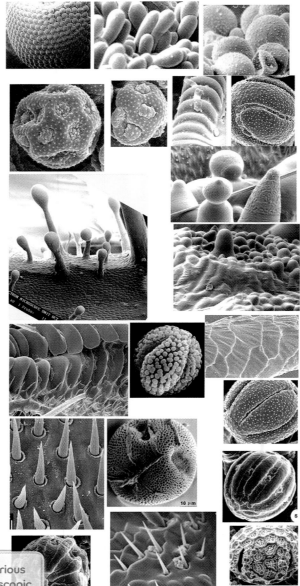

50+ mspf (81)

500+ batches (750)

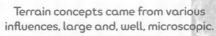
An early version of a planetscape showing the terrain and flora

Terrain concepts came from various influences, large and, well, microscopic.

Planet Concepts

The design of planets in *Spore* was a serious business. In addition to the scripted planets, several thematic planet concepts were proposed, and some of the coolest concept art developed. Many of these concept sketches and paintings, as well as quite a few other pieces of concept art, were produced by Christian Scheurer (Concept Artist) and Shannon Galvin (Artist).

INDUSTRIAL
WASTE-LAND

LEVELATED
CITIES

ANDROMEDA
STILT CITY

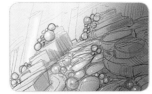

CRABLEG PLANET

SPACE VIEW

IN A WORLD WHERE LIFE NO LONGER HAS MEANING..
A WORLD WHERE CORPORATE GREED FIGHTS AGAINST
THE VERY SPIRIT OF FREEDOM, ONE MAN MUST STAND
ALONE TO FIGHT AGAINST TYRANNY.
THIS IS SHITAAKE MOON.

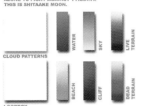

CLOUD PATTERNS

WATER | SKY | LIVE TERRAIN

LOOPBOX PARTICLES

BEACH | CLIFF | DEAD TERRAIN

CIVILIZATION VIEW

LAND SCRIPT

SCRIPT & DECAL
GOES UNDER CLAW

ROCK SETS

MASSIVE ROCKS

LARGE ROCKS

MEDIUM ROCKS

SMALL ROCKS

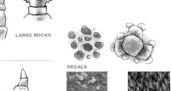

DECALS

GROUND TEXTURES | GRASS TYPES

SUGGESTED FLORA TYPES
(Decidious or large leaves. Nothing spikey
that would get confused with the rock types)

SHITAAKE MOON

SPACE VIEW

IN A WORLD WHERE LIFE NO LONGER HAS MEANING..
A WORLD WHERE CORPORATE GREED FIGHTS AGAINST
THE VERY SPIRIT OF FREEDOM, ONE MAN MUST STAND
ALONE TO FIGHT AGAINST TYRANNY.
THIS IS SHITAAKE MOON.

CLOUD PATTERNS

WATER | SKY | LIVE TERRAIN

LOOPBOX PARTICLES

BEACH | CLIFF | DEAD TERRAIN

LAND SCRIPT

CIVILIZATION VIEW

SCRIPT TO GO UNDER
MASSIVE OBJECT

ROCK SETS

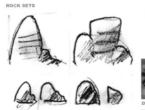

FLORA

DECALS

GROUND TEXTURES

GRASS TYPES

Early Terrain System Planet Creations

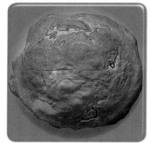

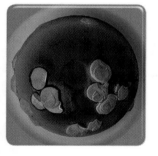

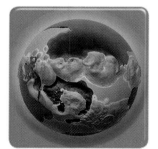

The User Interface

We decided it was okay to start simple with the User Interface.... We had to make sure if we are adding to it, we weren't just changing things around and making it more complex for no reason.

—Susie Moutray, User Interface Art & Design

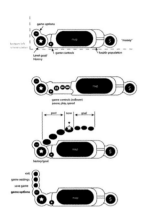

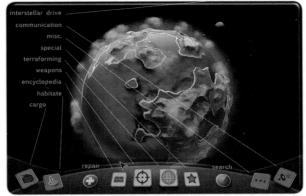

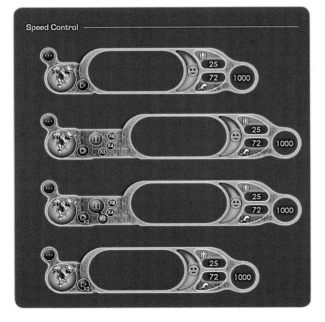

I might get inspiration for user interface design not only from other games, but by looking at the way iPod works, a copy machine, the dashboard of a car, just little things like that. The microwave, the iPhone—all kinds of things inspire me.

—Renaud Ternynck, Lead User Interface Art & Design

MECHANIC

DIETY COMPLEX

HERO

ZOOLOGIST
create # of food webs

TRAVELER

TERRA WRANGLER

DIPLOMAT

CLEANER
(kill sick aliens)

GOPHER
(fetch missions)

COLLECTOR

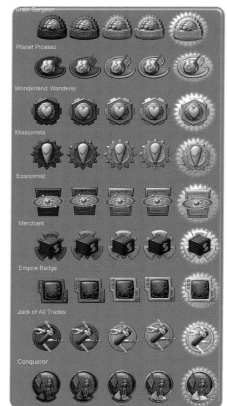

Brain Surgeon

Planet Picasso

Wonderland Wanderer

Missionista

Economist

Merchant

Empire Badge

Jack of All Trades

Conqueror

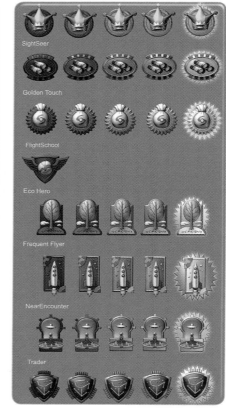

SightSeer

Golden Touch

FlightSchool

Eco Hero

Frequent Flyer

NearEncounter

Trader

COLONIST BADGE

WARMONGER BADGE

EXPLORER BADGE

MASTER BADGE

COLLECTOR BADGE

With the badges in the Space game, we make sure that we are meeting all the different play styles. So there will be the explorer players, the colonizers, the collectors, the terraformers, the warmongers.

—KIP KATSARELIS,
PRODUCER: GAMEPLAY

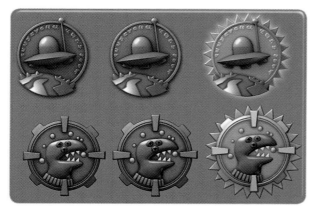

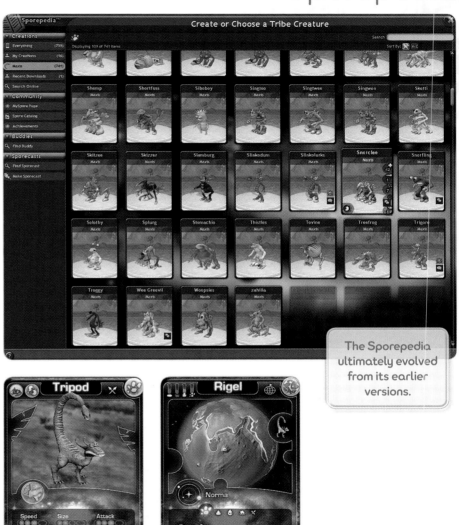

Labels on top-left diagram:

- Sort
- Preview
- All feeds
- Favorite feeds
- Account and preference.
  Would include blocked content management
- Polinated content
- Search Feeds
- Content
- Community
- Filtered content
  - My Creations — 12
  - Feeds — 6
  - Buddies — 8
  - Suggestions
- Favorites
- Filtered Favorites
  - Favorites
  - Star City
  - Bartertown
  - Star Wars Theme
- Create new list
- Sharing indicator
- Feeds
- Name — Creator — Date
- Will's World — 150 items
- Lost World — 20 items
- *the* list — 32 items
- Serena's top 50 — 50 items
- Spormaniac — 84 items
- Le Spore — 45 items
- Queue
- Priority — Kind
- Current game
- Queue fully managable Queue
  - 1 Housing
  - 2 Housing
  - 3 Flora
  - 4 Plop
  - 5 Rhinus
  - 6 Factory
  - 7 Temple
  - 8 Farm
- Update Queue
- Update Queue

Early approaches to the Sporepedia were called the "Multiverse." Here are some examples of the first attempts.

The players as they create creatures or buildings or cities or planets can name them, and they will be shared amongst players. But you know it's funny, when you just attach a name to something, how much time people will spend sitting there thinking about what to name it. Because at that point it really kind of crystallizes in their mind. At first they made this pretty picture, then they name it and then, ooh. What does it look like? Well, it looks like Bozo. Maybe Bozo lives on the planet of so and so, and they actually start naturally in their head expanding the narrative possibility space around that thing.

—WILL WRIGHT, SPORE VISION & CHIEF DESIGNER

The Sporepedia ultimately evolved from its earlier versions.

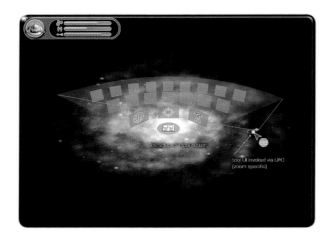

The early version of the Sporepedia was called the Encyclopedia Galactica.

We built an infinite content machine. You make content and share content and use content, and these features are not stuck someplace over on the side; they're integral to the game.

—ALEX HUTCHINSON, LEAD DESIGNER: GAMEPLAY

Well, we have only had a limited number of people interact with it, in focus tests that we do, and our own team members. Our idea was to start with the small group we have here, building stuff in the creators. It always surprises me what they can do. But everything I've done, I've always been totally surprised with what the players have ended up doing with it. They have always exceeded my expectations, in almost every dimension, and that's dealing with tools that are an order of magnitude less powerful than what we're building now. So I have no doubt they are going to continue to entertain us, and that's the fun part. We spend all this time trying to entertain them, and then we ship it and they start entertaining us.

—WILL WRIGHT, *SPORE* VISION & CHIEF DESIGNER

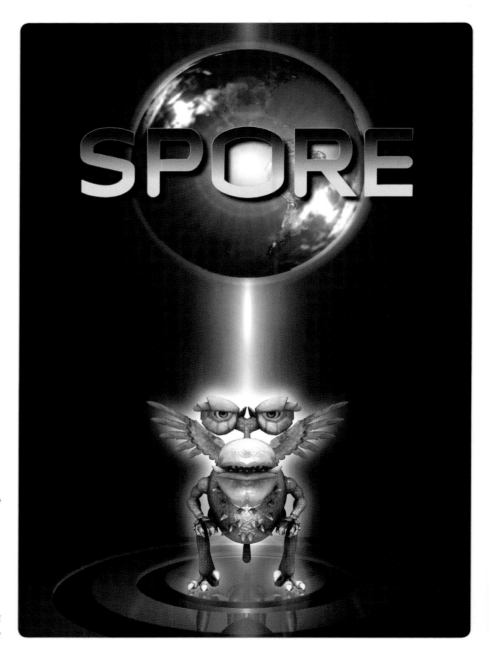

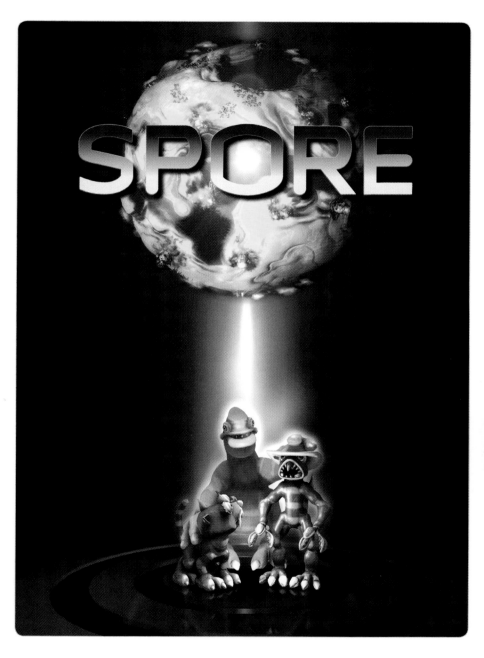

SPORE

The part for me that's the payoff of all of this—I mean, there's a ton of crazy cool technology going on underneath the hood, but I still get shivers up my spine when I watch a video or watch someone do it when they first pop a mouth on the thing and it goes "Rwaark" or "Eeerrr," you know. It's like, "Whoa! That's just so cool." Every time. And the number of things that have to come together, like stuff that I did and stuff that Ocean did and stuff that everyone on the team did, like the creator guys making it possible—it's a big team effort to make this thing come alive. And then it will dance a little jig and point at you or something. It's totally absurdly cool. I mean, it's magic. It's just never happened in the game industry before. It's awesome.

I just can't wait to see what the players make. They're going to be a hundred times—a million times more creative than us. It's going to be the wild west. The themes are going to be great. And great stuff is going to bubble up, you know, like Web 2.0 style. And you'll wonder, like I bet there's stuff in there that nobody's ever seen, and you'll go spelunking in there and try and find it.

And the cool thing about user-created content and games like that is it totally turns it into a meritocracy—like whoever can make the coolest creature wins, right?

What is the secret of life? It's for me to know and you to find out.

... It flattens everything out. It's like, if Will doesn't make the coolest creature, it doesn't bubble to the top, and it doesn't matter if you're like "famous guy." And some people will become famous for making the greatest *Spore* creations.
—Chris Hecker, Design & Lead Engineer: Procedural Animation

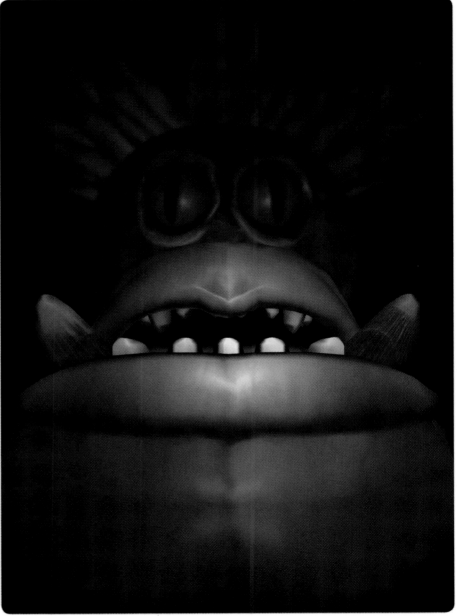

Acknowledgments

First, I have to acknowledge Will Wright. Will is a humble genius, a perpetual kid playing with concepts as diverse as organic chemistry and astrobiology, the habits of ants and people, architecture, the origin of the universe, and the meaning of life. His dry sense of humor and brilliant insights make him a joy to spend time with. I thank Will for giving me the opportunity to work on this book.

Second, I want to thank Brodie Andersen, who got the dubious honor of being my go-between at Maxis. Brodie was amazing, pulling together everything I needed, arranging interviews, securing artwork, and finding answers to all my questions—and always with a smile. Without Brodie, I honestly don't know how this book would have gotten done.

I also want to thank Ocean Quigley. Ocean has been a friend of mine and colleague for many years, and was always willing to let me trade upon that friendship to offer help when I needed something extra for the book. Ocean is an amazing artist, a deep thinker, and an even better friend.

There are, of course, many more people to thank. Bob King for creating the *Astounding Spore Tales* for this book. Alex, Chris, Christian, Dan, Grue, Holly, Jason, Jenna, John, Kate, Kip, Lucy, Matt, Mike, Renaud, Shannon, Soren, and Susie for providing the real text for this book through the interviews. And Chaim for providing some thoughtful essays from which I have quoted. Also, thanks to those whose artistic contributions are visible within these pages—Umaru, Eddy, Gal, Tony, Zach, Jane, and Matt. I also want to thank my friend and colleague Paul Lipscombe for help with transcribing the *Spore* team interviews. I want to offer my special thanks to Lucy Bradshaw. I've known Lucy for years, and I know that having a journalist poking around your offices and talking to your team members can be a distraction, and a headache for a conscientious producer. So thanks for putting up with me yet again, Lucy. And finally, thanks to Darren Montgomery for helping spearhead the project as liaison between Maxis and Prima.

—Rusel DeMaria